TOGETHER

TOGETHER

OUR COMMUNITY COOKBOOK

THE HUBB COMMUNITY KITCHEN

PHOTOGRAPHY BY
JENNY ZARINS

EBURY
PRESS

Dedication

This book is dedicated to all those whose lives
were impacted by the fire at Grenfell Tower.

CONTENTS

FOREWORD

Together is more than a cookbook. This is a tale of friendship, and a story of togetherness. It is a homage to the power of cooking as a community, and the recipes that allow us to connect, share and look forward.

In January 2018, as I was settling in to my new home of London, it was important to me to get to know organisations working in the local community. I made a quiet trip to Al-Manaar, a mosque close to the Grenfell community.

In 2017, I had watched the Grenfell Tower tragedy unfold on the news; I was in Canada at the time, sharing the global sentiment of shock and sympathy for what this community was enduring, while also deeply wanting to help. Fast-forward seven months, and I was set to meet some of the women affected by the fire, at a community kitchen in Al-Manaar.

The kitchen was opened after the Grenfell tragedy, offering women who had been displaced and the community around them a space to cook food for their families. Their roles as matriarchs united them across their cultures; the kitchen provided an opportunity to cook what they knew and to taste the memory of home, albeit homes some had recently lost.

The kitchen buzzes with women of all ages; women who have lived and seen life; laughing, chatting, sharing a cup of tea and a story, while children play on the floor or are rocked to sleep in their strollers. Now I have come to know these women and this place well, here are a few things to note about the community kitchen:

It is cosy and brightly lit, with scents of cardamom, curry
and ginger dancing through the air.

It will take you about fifteen minutes to enter the room, as you will be joyfully greeted
by kisses (cheek x 3) by each of the incredible women there.

You will find yourself in a melting pot of cultures and personalities, who have roots
in Uganda, Iraq, Morocco, India, Russia and at least ten other countries.

You should undoubtedly arrive on an empty stomach because upon departure
you will have been stuffed to the gills with samosas flecked with cinnamon, chapatis
flavoured with carrots and onion, Russian Semolina cake, Persian teas and my very
favourite avocado dip that I now make at home.

You will feel joyful in their company, and you will leave counting
the days until you go back.

On my first visit, I asked Munira, the resident *chef de cuisine* (so to speak), how I could help. An apron was quickly wrapped around me, I pushed up my sleeves, and I found myself washing the rice for lunch. Munira's sister-in-law, who had flown in from Egypt after Grenfell to help the family, helped me divide the correct amount of butter and fresh thyme to pour into the pot of rice bubbling away on the stovetop. All the aromas percolating in a kitchen filled with countless languages aflutter, remains one of my most treasured memories from my first visit to the kitchen.

I have a lifelong interest in the story of food – where it comes from, why we embrace it and how it brings us together: the universal connection to community through the breaking of bread. Within this kitchen's walls, there exists not only the communal bond of togetherness through sharing food, but also a cultural diversity that creates what I would describe as a passport on a plate: the power of a meal to take you to places you've never been, or transport you right back to where you came from.

One of my own favourite meals is collard greens, black-eyed peas and cornbread – a meal I would look forward to throughout my childhood: the smell of yellow onions simmering amongst a slow-cooked pot of greens from my grandma's back garden; the earthy texture of peas; and a golden loaf of cornbread puff-puffing away to a browned peak in the warmth of the oven. This was always eaten on New Year's Day, a tradition steeped in ancestral history where each component has a meaning: the black-eyed peas for prosperity, the greens for wealth, the cornbread for health and nourishment. It wasn't a new year's resolution; it was a wish. It wasn't simply a meal; it was a story.

I've spent many years away from my birthplace of Los Angeles and have found that travelling far from home highlights the power of personally meaningful recipes. During my time at university in Chicago I would wait with bated breath to return to LA for the winter break and have a bowl of my mother's gumbo. And while living in Toronto (seven years of being adopted by that beautiful place for work), I embraced poutine and several other Canadian culinary favourites, but the Southern California girl in me always craved fish tacos, and the memory of eating hometown fare infused with a strong Mexican influence.

We've all had that experience where you have a bite of food, close your eyes, and taste, remember and even feel the first time you enjoyed it. There is good reason that chicken soup is often credited with healing not just a cold, but the soul. There is something quintessentially restorative about a taste of something meaningful.

I immediately felt connected to this community kitchen; it is a place for women to laugh, grieve, cry and cook together. Melding cultural identities under a shared roof, it creates a space to feel a sense of normality – in its simplest form, the universal need to connect, nurture and commune through food, through crisis or joy – something we can all relate to.

During my visit I met Zahira, a working mum who oversees much of the coordination at Al-Manaar and whose infectious smile is enough to make you forget any troubles. Upon learning the kitchen was only open on Tuesdays and Thursdays I asked, 'Why isn't this open seven days a week?'

Her response: 'Funding.'

And now just a few months later, here we are… Together.

Through this charitable endeavour, the proceeds will allow the kitchen to thrive and keep the global spirit of community alive. With the support of dynamic women from all walks of life, we have come together with a united vision to empower other women to share their stories through food. This cookbook is a celebration of life, community and the impact of coming together.

Our hope is that within these pages you will find new recipes and family favourites that you can enjoy in your own homes, because these recipes aren't simply meals; they are stories of family, love, of survival and of connection. From a Thanksgiving supper to a Shabbat dinner or a Sunday roast, the meals that bring us together are the meals that allow us to grow, to listen, to engage and to be present. We invite you to do the same, *together*, in your home, communities and beyond.

Great thanks to everyone who made this book possible. And thanks to you, the reader, for supporting the good work of the Hubb Community Kitchen.

Now it's time…
to gather, Together.

HRH The Duchess of Sussex

INTRODUCTION

Our kitchen has always been a place of good food, love, support and friendship. We cook the recipes we've grown up with; there's no stress, and the recipes always work because they have been made so many times – it's proper comfort food. Cakes, stews and spicy dips have become some of our favourite weekly dishes.

A love of cooking and sharing food brought us together after the Grenfell fire. Swapping family recipes and moments of laughter gave us a sense of normality and home. We named ourselves the Hubb Community Kitchen to celebrate the thing that we all feel every time we meet – *hubb* means 'love' in Arabic.

One day in January we had a surprise visit from Meghan; she cooked with us, and asked why the kitchen was only open two days a week. We replied, 'funding'. We thought she was joking when she said, 'well, how about making a cookbook?' But here we are, publishing *Together*, which will help to keep the kitchen open as long as we need it.

As everyone who was affected by the fire in 2017 settles into their new lives, we will continue to share the blessings of food made with love with those around us. And we hope that other people and communities can experience the healing power of sharing food by setting up their own local kitchens.

But the thing we want most is for you to enjoy cooking these recipes at home with your families. Each dish has a story, some handed down from generation to generation. We hope that by making them, and serving them, you will weave your own stories in with ours, creating a connection across our countries and cultures.

THE WOMEN OF THE HUBB COMMUNITY KITCHEN

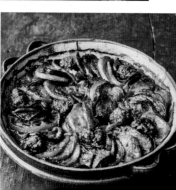

BREAKFASTS

SHAKSHOUKA

My father's family owned olive presses in Algeria. When he came back from business trips, he brought with him oil that was as green as grass – quite unlike anything we'd seen before. He used to make this special breakfast for us to celebrate his return. Cook peppers, tomatoes and onions, add courgettes if you like, break in some eggs and eat with flatbread. Delicious!

SERVES 4

2 tbsp olive oil

2 onions, finely chopped

2 green peppers, cored, de-
seeded and finely sliced

2 garlic cloves, grated

½ tsp cumin seeds

1 tbsp tomato purée

7 ripe vine tomatoes,
roughly chopped
(or 1 x 400g tin chopped
tomatoes)

75ml water

4 eggs

salt and pepper

flatbreads and Greek
yoghurt, to serve

Heat the oil in a deep frying pan on a medium–high heat. When hot, add the onions and peppers and fry for about 10 minutes, stirring often, until soft and lightly coloured.

Add the garlic and cook for 2 minutes, then add the cumin seeds and tomato purée and cook for 2 minutes until fragrant.

Add the tomatoes and water and simmer for 10 minutes or until the tomatoes have broken down and the mixture has thickened slightly. Season with salt and pepper to taste.

Make four small hollows in the mixture and crack an egg into each. Gently simmer until the egg whites are cooked, but the yolks remain runny, 15–20 minutes.

Serve from the pan, along with flatbreads and Greek yoghurt.

BARLEY PORRIDGE WITH FRUIT & NUTS

My Lebanese husband is a real gym freak and likes to eat healthily, so I look for lower-fat versions of the traditional dishes from our cultures. I love anything made with couscous, so this porridge fits the bill for both of us. And you don't have to stand over a pan stirring on busy mornings. I vary the amount of water – I prefer a firm texture, but Hussein has it more like normal porridge.

SERVES 4

150g barley couscous
  (*belboula*)
2 tsp olive or vegetable oil
300ml boiling water
½ tsp ground cinnamon,
  or to taste
75g walnut halves
150g blueberries
75g fresh pomegranate
  seeds
4 small fresh figs, quartered
  (optional)
200ml milk or almond milk,
  to serve

Place the couscous in a large bowl. Add the oil and mix with a fork until all the grains are coated. Add the boiling water, cover with clingfilm and leave for 10 minutes. When all the water has been absorbed, fluff up the couscous with a fork and add the cinnamon to taste.

To serve, pile the couscous into a large serving dish or individual bowls and smooth over the surface. Decorate with the walnuts, blueberries, pomegranate seeds and figs (if using), or with other toppings of your choice.

Serve the milk or almond milk on the side, to be stirred in according to taste.

MOROCCAN PANCAKES WITH HONEY & ALMOND BUTTER

I grew up in France, so to me pancakes meant delicate French crêpes. But then I discovered these delicious breakfast pancakes on a trip to my mother's homeland, Morocco. They are made without oil, so are very low in fat. *Amlou* contains argan oil – an amazing Moroccan ingredient often used in cosmetics; its unique nutty flavour makes this sweet dairy-free spread quite extraordinary. Of course, when I am short of time we have the pancakes with jam instead.

MAKES 12 PANCAKES

For the pancakes
150g fine semolina
75g self-raising flour
3.5g fast-action dried yeast
    (half of a 7g sachet)
½ tsp baking powder
1 tsp caster sugar
pinch of salt
375ml warm water

For the amlou *(honey and*
    almond butter)
4 tbsp almond butter
3 tbsp runny honey
1 tsp culinary argan oil
    (available in health food
    stores, good supermarkets
    and online)

Put all the pancake ingredients in a large mixing bowl and whisk well to make a smooth batter. Cover loosely with clingfilm and leave for about 45 minutes, until plenty of bubbles have formed and the batter has risen.

Meanwhile, put the *amlou* ingredients in a small bowl and mix with a spoon to combine; set aside.

Heat a non-stick frying pan on a low–medium heat; when it's hot, add a small ladleful of batter to the pan. Cook the pancake for 3–4 minutes, until the surface has lots of bubbles and has dried. Do not flip; transfer to kitchen paper and repeat with the rest of the batter, making a total of 12 pancakes. Let the pancakes cool slightly before you stack them, or they may stick together.

Serve warm, drizzled with the *amlou*.

GREEN OMELETTE

I'm a big fan of eggs for breakfast. I make this omelette filled with mushrooms and green herbs to give my two daughters a good start before a day at school. As for the cream... I can't help it. It's the Russian in me: we add cream to everything.

MAKES 4 OMELETTES

5 tbsp unsalted butter

200g button mushrooms, thinly sliced

16 eggs

4 tbsp single cream

20g fresh chives, chopped

25g fresh parsley, chopped

150g mature Cheddar cheese, coarsely grated

salt and pepper

Heat 1 tablespoon of the butter in a non-stick frying pan on a medium–high heat. Add the mushrooms and fry for 4–5 minutes until cooked and golden. Transfer to a plate and set aside.

Add the eggs, cream, chives, parsley and some salt and pepper to a large jug or mixing bowl and whisk with a fork to combine.

Heat 1 tablespoon of the butter in the same pan on a medium heat. Once the butter has melted and is starting to gently sizzle, pour in a quarter of the egg mix. Swirl the pan so the egg mix reaches the edges and then leave it to cook for 5–7 minutes.

Add a quarter of the fried mushrooms and a quarter of the cheese to one side of the omelette. Fold the other side over the mushrooms and cheese, then cover the pan with a lid and cook for 3 minutes. Transfer to a plate and repeat the process to make four omelettes in total. Serve immediately.

AFRICAN BEIGNETS

We can all do with a little pleasure in our lives. *Mahamri* are light and fluffy buns, rather like doughnuts, and are good with cream cheese, honey or jam, although in Uganda we eat them with everything, even meat.

MAKES 12 BEIGNETS

140g plain flour, plus extra
    for dusting
210g self-raising flour
3.5g fast-action dried yeast
    (half of a 7g sachet)
75g caster sugar
¼ tsp ground cardamom
1 egg, beaten
120ml coconut milk
1 tbsp ghee, melted
1 tsp vegetable oil, plus
    extra for greasing
jam, honey or cream cheese,
    to serve

Place the flours, yeast, sugar and cardamom in a mixing bowl. Mix thoroughly using your fingers.

Make a hollow in the middle of the dry ingredients and pour in the egg, coconut milk and melted ghee. Working with your fingers, gently incorporate the flour into the liquid until it comes together and forms a soft dough. Add a tablespoon of water if needed.

Knead the dough for 10 minutes, until smooth and stretchy. Rub the oil between your hands and smooth this oil around the dough. Place in a lightly oiled bowl, cover with clingfilm and leave to rise for a couple of hours, depending on the temperature of your kitchen, until doubled in size.

Preheat the oven to 180°C. Line a baking sheet with baking paper.

Divide the dough into three equal balls. On a worktop lightly dusted with flour, roll each ball into a 15cm circle, cut each circle into quarters and place them on the prepared baking sheet. Cover with clingfilm and leave to rise slightly for 30 minutes.

Bake the beignets for 12–15 minutes, until puffed and golden. Serve with jam, honey or cream cheese, or as you prefer.

NOTE Instead of baking, you can shallow fry the beignets for 3–4 minutes, turning them regularly.

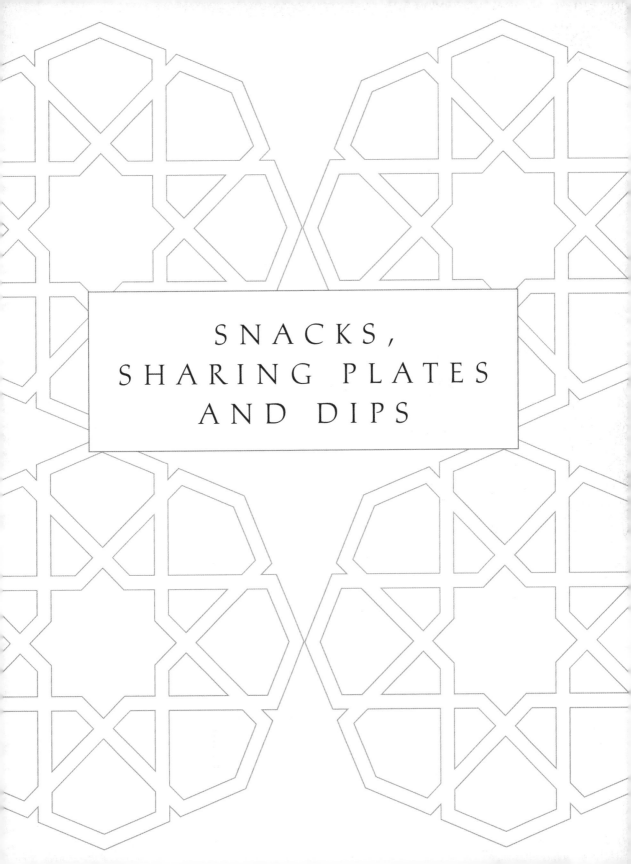

SNACKS, SHARING PLATES AND DIPS

KOFTA KEBABS WITH ONION & SUMAC PICKLE

I grew up in Yemen, one of nine children. My Mum's life's work was raising her family and she used to make these kebabs to fill up me and my siblings. You can grill the kebabs or cook them in the oven – but as my Mum was often in a hurry, particularly with six hungry growing boys, she used to quickly fry them and they would eat them straight out of the pan.

MAKES 12 KOFTAS
SERVES 4

20g fresh breadcrumbs
3 tbsp water
1 small onion,
    roughly chopped
2 garlic cloves, peeled
10g fresh parsley
500g minced beef
250g minced lamb
1 tsp ground allspice
½ tsp ground cardamom
½ tsp sumac (see page 90)
½ tsp freshly grated nutmeg
½ tsp paprika
1 tsp salt
½ tsp freshly ground
    black pepper
vegetable oil, for brushing
pitta breads and Romaine
    lettuce leaves, to serve

For the onion and
    sumac pickle
1 large red or yellow onion,
    thinly sliced
1 tbsp white wine vinegar
½ tsp sumac (see page 90),
    plus extra to serve

Soak 12 bamboo skewers (about 18cm long) in water for at least 30 minutes.

To make the pickle, mix the onion slices with the vinegar in a large bowl. Sprinkle with the sumac and set aside for at least 10 minutes. Sprinkle with a little more sumac when ready to serve.

Mix the breadcrumbs with the water and leave for 5 minutes.

Put the onion, garlic and parsley in a food processor and pulse three or four times until finely chopped but not puréed. Add the beef, lamb, soaked breadcrumbs, spices, salt and pepper. Process until well mixed and paste-like.

Alternatively, if you don't have a food processor, finely chop the onion, garlic and parsley and place in a mixing bowl. Add the meat, soaked breadcrumbs and the spices and knead by hand until well blended.

Divide the meat mixture into 12 portions. Mould each portion around a bamboo skewer. Place on a tray lined with baking paper.

Heat a griddle pan until hot. Lightly brush the koftas with oil and grill for 8–9 minutes, in two batches, turning them halfway, until cooked through.

Serve with pitta breads, the onion and sumac pickle and lettuce.

NOTE You can also cook the koftas on a barbecue.

EGYPTIAN LAMB FATTAH

✱✱✱
✱✱✱ My husband was born in Grenfell; his was one of the first families to move in. I learned
✱✱✱ how to make this dish from his mother. It's traditional to serve it at Eid, the festival
that marks the end of Ramadan. Don't worry if you can't find gum mastic (dried resin used
as flavouring, sold in Middle Eastern shops and online); the dish works just as well without.

SERVES 4

7 tbsp ghee or vegetable oil

2 onions, roughly chopped

900g lamb neck fillet or
    boneless lamb shoulder,
    cut into 2.5cm pieces

½ tsp gum mastic (optional)

8 cardamom pods, crushed

2 bay leaves

1 litre chicken stock

300g Egyptian short grain
    rice or long grain rice

850ml water

3 pitta breads

1 tbsp crushed garlic

5 tbsp tomato purée

½ tsp ground cumin

1 tbsp white wine vinegar

salt and pepper

Heat 3 tablespoons of the ghee/oil in a large sauté pan on a medium heat and fry the onions for 5 minutes, until soft but not golden. Add the lamb and fry for 10 minutes, until lightly browned. Add the gum mastic (if using), cardamom and bay leaves, followed by the stock. Season with salt and pepper, bring to the boil and skim off the foam on the surface. Lower the heat, cover and gently simmer for 1 hour (or 1½ hours if using lamb shoulder), until tender.

Meanwhile, wash the rice until the water runs clear, then drain.

Heat 2 tablespoons of the ghee/oil in a heavy-based pan on a medium heat. Add the rice and stir until all the grains are coated. Add 450ml of the water and bring to the boil. Stir in ½ teaspoon of salt. Turn the heat to the lowest setting, cover and cook for 25–30 minutes, until the water has been absorbed and the rice is tender.

Preheat the oven to 200°C. Line a large baking sheet with baking paper. Split the pitta breads horizontally into two thin halves, then tear or cut them into bite-sized pieces. Spread on the baking sheet and bake for 10–12 minutes, turning them halfway through, until golden brown and crisp.

Heat the remaining ghee/oil in a pan on a medium heat. Fry the garlic until lightly golden. Add the tomato purée and fry for 2–3 minutes, stirring. Add the cumin and vinegar and stir for a few seconds. Add the remaining 400ml of water, stir until well blended, season and simmer for 15 minutes until reduced and thickened.

To assemble: spread the baked pitta pieces on a serving platter, top with the rice, then add the lamb and some stock from the pan. Drizzle some tomato sauce over the top. Serve with extra stock and tomato sauce on the side.

INTLAK ALSAIEGH'S *Kubba Haleb*

IRAQI LAMB CROQUETTES

I've worked at Al-Manaar since 2001 and have seen the power of food in creating a welcoming atmosphere. People of different nationalities are sometimes fearful of each other – sharing food helps them to relax and the bonds of friendship are made. These meat-filled croquettes are something I make whenever we have guests. We never make small quantities: we cook for large numbers and we put all the food on the table at the same time.

MAKES 30 KUBBA

375g basmati rice, soaked in
    cold water for 30 minutes,
    then rinsed and drained
1 tbsp ground turmeric
300ml water
salt and pepper

For the filling
1 tbsp olive oil
1 small onion, finely
    chopped
450g minced lamb (20% fat)
2½ tbsp *baharat*
    (Lebanese seven-spice
    mix; see page 34)
40g raisins, roughly chopped
25g pine nuts
2–3 tbsp chopped fresh
    parsley
1–2 tbsp sunflower oil

NOTE If you don't want to cook all the *kubba* at once, freeze once moulded and use within 1 month (defrost thoroughly before cooking).

Put the rice in a pan, add the turmeric and a generous pinch of salt. Pour in the water and stir well. Bring to the boil, reduce the heat, cover with a lid and simmer for 20–25 minutes, until the water has been absorbed. Remove the pan from the heat, keeping the lid on, and set aside for 30 minutes. Do not lift the lid.

Meanwhile, heat the oil in a large frying pan on a medium heat and cook the onion for 5 minutes or until soft. Increase the heat, add the lamb and a little salt and pepper and cook for 5 minutes, until browned, breaking up the mince as it cooks. Stir in the *baharat*, raisins and pine nuts, and fry for another 5 minutes until the lamb is cooked through (add up to 2 tablespoons of water if the mixture seems dry). Remove the pan from the heat, taste and adjust the seasoning if needed and leave to cool. Stir through the parsley.

Transfer the cooled rice to a food processor and pulse to form a tacky dough (leave some grains intact for texture). If the rice has dried out slightly, gradually add up to 2 tablespoons of water and briefly pulse again. When you reach the desired consistency, transfer to a bowl.

Line a baking sheet with baking paper. Weigh out 25g of the rice dough. With wet hands, roll the dough into a ball, then use your thumb to flatten into a disc in the palm of your hand. Place 15g of the lamb filling in the centre of the disc and bring the edges of the dough together to encase the lamb, gently moulding it into an oval torpedo shape. Repeat with the rest of the dough and lamb filling, placing them on the lined baking sheet. Let them sit for 30 minutes.

Preheat the oven to 200°C. Brush the *kubba* with sunflower oil, then bake on the top shelf of the oven for 20 minutes. Serve immediately.

SPICED POTATO KIBBEH

This mix of potato and bulgur wheat was always on our table back in Baghdad. Moist on the inside, crispy on the outside, it goes with just about anything. You can find the *baharat* spice mix in Middle Eastern food shops and some supermarkets, or you can make your own (see below). This makes about 4 tablespoons: enough for all the recipes in the book. It will keep for 6 months in an airtight container.

SERVES 4

500g floury potatoes, peeled and quartered

175g fine bulgur wheat

2 spring onions, finely chopped

¼ tsp paprika

¼ tsp *baharat* (Lebanese seven-spice mix; see below)

¼ tsp ground cumin

25g pine nuts, toasted (see page 127)

2 tbsp plain flour

3 tbsp olive oil, plus extra for greasing

salt and pepper

For the **Baharat** *spice mix*

1 tbsp ground cinnamon

1½ tsp ground cumin

1½ tsp ground coriander

1½ tsp ground allspice

1½ tsp freshly ground black pepper

1½ tsp paprika

¼ tsp freshly grated nutmeg

¼ tsp ground cloves

⅛ tsp ground cardamom

If making your own *baharat* spice mix, simply mix all the spices until well blended. Store in an airtight container.

Put the potatoes in a pan, cover with cold water and bring to the boil. Add 1 teaspoon of salt and cook for 20–30 minutes or until tender when pierced with a knife.

Meanwhile, soak the bulgur wheat in cold water for 10 minutes, then drain, tip onto a piece of cheesecloth and squeeze dry.

Preheat the oven to 180°C. Brush a 23cm shallow cake or tart tin with olive oil.

When the potatoes are cooked, drain in a colander and place the colander back in the pan for 5 minutes. The steam from the hot pan will help dry the potatoes.

While the potatoes are still warm, press them through a ricer into a large bowl. Add the bulgur wheat, spring onions, spices, nuts and flour and mix until thoroughly combined.

Firmly press the mixture into the oiled cake/tart tin: it should be about 2.5cm thick. Score the top into eight portions and make a 1cm hole in the centre. Drizzle with the olive oil and bake for 30–40 minutes or until the top is golden and crisp. Leave to cool before serving.

POTATO FRITTERS WITH CORIANDER CHUTNEY

I work at Al-Manaar and on the day of the Grenfell disaster I helped cook for 200 people – it was the first time I'd ever cooked for anyone outside my family. My Mum, who is from Mumbai, used to make these fritters for us. They're very tasty – put them on the table and they'll vanish in an instant.

MAKES 10 FRITTERS

SERVES 4-6

1 tbsp olive oil

20g fresh root ginger, peeled and grated

1 green chilli, de-seeded and finely chopped

¼ tsp ground turmeric

5g fresh coriander, chopped

450g mashed potato

juice of ½ lemon

2 tsp caster sugar

1.5 litres sunflower oil

salt

For the batter

150g gram flour

¼ tsp chilli powder

¼ tsp asafoetida

½ tsp bicarbonate of soda

1 tbsp olive oil

180ml water

For the coriander chutney

75g fresh coriander

3 garlic cloves, peeled

4 green chillies, de-seeded

60g *nylon sev* (see note)

7 tbsp water

1 tsp ground cumin

Heat the olive oil in a large frying pan on a medium–high heat. When hot, add the ginger, chilli, turmeric and coriander and fry for 1 minute. Add the mashed potato, lemon juice, sugar and a pinch of salt, mix well and sauté on a medium heat for 3–4 minutes. Taste to check for seasoning, then transfer to a plate, spread out and leave to cool for 20 minutes.

Meanwhile, add the batter ingredients to a mixing bowl and whisk to form a smooth batter. Transfer to the fridge to rest until needed.

To make the chutney, put the coriander, garlic, chillies and *nylon sev* into a food processor and blitz until well combined, gradually adding the water until you reach the desired consistency. Stir through the cumin and ¼ teaspoon of salt, taste to check for seasoning and set aside.

Divide the cooled potato mix into ten equal pieces and roll into balls. Place back on the plate and transfer to the fridge for 25 minutes to firm up the potato before coating and frying.

Fill a large heavy-based saucepan or deep-fat fryer no more than two-thirds full with sunflower oil and heat to about 180°C. Gather the potato balls and batter from the fridge. Dip three of the balls in the batter, turn to coat completely and then very carefully place in the hot oil, using a slotted spoon or tongs. Gently push the fritters around in the oil to get an even colour, and fry for 3–4 minutes. Transfer to a plate lined with kitchen paper and repeat with the remaining balls, in batches.

Serve hot, with the coriander chutney.

NOTE *Nylon sev* are crisp little noodles made from gram flour and spices, sold in Indian stores and online.

STUFFED PEPPERS

 This is such a good sharing dish, especially if you have vegetarian guests. Just make sure they help themselves first, because the meat-eaters will all want some as well.

SERVES 4-6

150g feta cheese

3 garlic cloves, finely
    chopped

10g fresh parsley, chopped

1 tsp freshly ground
    black pepper

8 romano peppers

4 tbsp olive oil

crusty bread, to serve

Preheat the oven to 180°C.

Place the feta, garlic, parsley and black pepper in a mixing bowl and mash together with the back of a fork to form a paste.

Cut the stalk ends off the peppers, then carefully de-seed. Stuff each pepper with the feta mix, using a small spoon to push it down into the cavity. Brush the peppers all over with 1 tablespoon of the oil.

Transfer the stuffed peppers to a large baking dish, so they fit together quite tightly, and spoon over the remaining oil. Bake for 35–40 minutes, until soft and beginning to char.

Serve hot with fresh crusty bread.

VEGETABLE SAMOSAS

Grenfell was a real community and my neighbour Rania and I used to party with food all the time. The first time I made these samosas for her, she ate 10 of them. Really! They look like a lot of work, but if you have a food processor to chop the vegetables it's very easy. Use my quick way of folding them too, to save time. Just be sure to make enough…

MAKES 12 SAMOSAS

1 potato, about 150g
3 tbsp vegetable oil, plus
    extra for brushing
1 tsp mustard seeds
¼ tsp fenugreek seeds
½ tsp cumin seeds
1 onion, finely sliced
½ tsp ground turmeric
½ tsp ground cinnamon
about 120g white cabbage,
    finely sliced
1 large carrot, about 120g,
    peeled and grated
100g mixed red and green
    peppers, cored, de-seeded
    and finely chopped
50g frozen peas
½ tsp granulated sugar
12 spring roll pastry
    wrappers, 25 x 25cm
1 egg, lightly beaten
salt

NOTE You can also make spring rolls with this filling. Filled samosas can be frozen for up to 8 weeks. Bake them from frozen for 20 minutes.

Boil the potato in salted water for 30 minutes until soft. Drain and leave to cool, then peel and dice.

Heat the vegetable oil in a large frying pan on a medium heat. Add the spice seeds and fry for 30 seconds, until fragrant. Add the onion and a pinch of salt and cook for about 2 minutes, until translucent. Add the turmeric and cinnamon and stir for a few seconds until the onion is coated with the spices. Add the cabbage, carrot and peppers and cook over high heat for 4–5 minutes or until soft.

Add the diced potato, peas, ½ teaspoon of salt and the sugar and stir for a couple of minutes. Taste and adjust the seasoning if needed. Transfer to a large plate or a tray and leave to cool.

Cut each pastry square in half to make two rectangles. Keep the pastry covered with a clean, damp tea towel to stop it drying out. Working with one strip of pastry at a time and with a long edge facing you, fold the bottom right-hand corner of the strip to meet the top edge, forming a triangle, then fold the top right-hand corner over to meet the top left-hand corner of the strip, forming a square. Brush the single layer of pastry (bottom left) with some beaten egg and fold over to form a triangular pouch. Open the pouch and fill with about 3 tablespoons of the samosa filling. Brush the triangular flap with beaten egg and fold over to seal the pouch. Place on a tray and keep covered while you make the rest of the samosas.

To bake the samosas, preheat the oven to 200°C and line a baking sheet with baking paper. Place the samosas on the baking sheet. Brush the tops with a little oil and then with some beaten egg. Bake for 10 minutes, then turn them over, brush the other side with oil and egg and bake for another 10 minutes.

ALGERIAN SWEET LAMB

In Algeria, this special dish is on the table every day during Ramadan. Although it's made with meat, it's very sweet from the dried fruits and you eat it last in the meal, like a dessert. It gives that moment of sweetness that rounds everything off.

SERVES 4-6

250g pitted prunes
150g dried apricots
100g dried figs, halved
25g sultanas
50g ghee or butter
1 onion, finely chopped
500g boneless lamb
shoulder, trimmed and
cut into 2cm pieces
2 cinnamon sticks
1 star anise
¼ tsp salt
250ml freshly made
strong tea
250ml boiling water
200g granulated sugar
1 tsp orange blossom water
flaked almonds, toasted (see
page 127), to garnish

Put the dried fruits into a bowl, add boiling water to cover and leave for 30 minutes.

Meanwhile, melt the ghee or butter in a large frying pan on a medium heat, add the onion and cook for 10 minutes, until golden. Add the lamb, cinnamon sticks, star anise and salt and fry for 12–15 minutes, until the lamb is well browned.

Add the tea, cover and simmer for 30 minutes or until reduced and thick.

Add the boiling water, sugar and orange blossom water and stir until the sugar has dissolved. Drain the soaked dried fruits, add to the pan and stir well. Simmer, uncovered, on a low–medium heat for 20 minutes, until the sauce has reduced and thickened, and the mixture is glossy.

Serve warm on small plates, garnished with toasted flaked almonds.

GREEN CHILLI & AVOCADO DIP

 My life-long dream has been to have a food van; I spend any free time I have thinking up dishes, and putting ingredients together in my mind. These dips are my own invention.

SERVES 4

2 green chillies, halved
   and de-seeded
25g fresh coriander
3 tbsp natural yoghurt
grated zest and juice of
   2 lemons
4 garlic cloves, peeled
flesh of 1 ripe avocado
4 tbsp mayonnaise
   (optional)
salt and pepper

Put all the ingredients except the mayonnaise into a food processor and blend until smooth. Taste and adjust the seasoning if necessary. Add mayonnaise (if you wish) and stir to combine, then transfer to a serving bowl.

MUNIRA MAHMUD'S

GREEN CHILLI & TOMATO DIP

 You can enjoy this dip with just about anything – it's quite spicy, but so tasty!

SERVES 4

2 green chillies, halved
   and de-seeded
½ onion, finely chopped
juice of 1 lemon
2 vine tomatoes, quartered
20g fresh coriander
salt and pepper

Blend all the ingredients together in a food processor. Taste and adjust the seasoning if necessary, then transfer to a serving bowl.

LEILA HEDJEM'S

TZATZIKI

I got this Greek recipe from my Irish Mum – but I don't know where she got it from! It's great in the summer because it's very cooling. Make it ahead of time and leave it in the fridge to let the flavours develop.

SERVES 4-6

1 cucumber, about 300g
400g natural Greek yoghurt
2 garlic cloves, grated
juice of ½ lemon
1 tbsp olive oil
salt and pepper

Peel the cucumber and halve lengthways. Scoop out the seeds with a spoon, then grate the flesh. Squeeze out the water from the grated flesh, then place in a bowl. Add the yoghurt, garlic, lemon juice, olive oil, and salt and pepper to taste; mix well to combine.

Chill in the fridge for 30 minutes before serving alongside pitta bread or grilled lamb.

LEILA HEDJEM'S

HUMMUS

I've always made my own hummus: it's so easy if you have a food processor. One day a Turkish friend told me to add fresh coriander – I've never looked back!
Pictured on page 49.

SERVES 4

4 tbsp tahini
juice of 1 lemon
2 garlic cloves, grated
1 x 400g tin chickpeas,
    drained and rinsed
3 tbsp olive oil, plus extra
    to drizzle
4½ tbsp water
10g fresh coriander, chopped
pinch of paprika
salt and pepper

Put the tahini and lemon juice in a food processor and blitz for about 30 seconds until combined. Add the garlic, chickpeas and olive oil and blitz until combined and thick. Gradually add the water until you reach the desired consistency. Season to taste, then fold through most of the chopped coriander.

Spoon into a serving bowl and top with a drizzle of olive oil, a pinch of paprika and the remaining coriander.

SPICY PEANUT DIP

✳✳✳ I wanted to cook something really typical from Uganda, where we often use ground nuts to make a peanut butter that we call *nino*. But our cuisine in the north of the country is quite spicy and I didn't think all the other ladies at the Hubb Kitchen would like it – so I made it into a dip to have on the side. Turns out it goes with just about everything!

SERVES 4-6

1 tbsp olive oil
1 onion, finely chopped
2 garlic cloves, crushed
1 tsp grated fresh root ginger
1 red chilli, finely chopped
1½ tsp ground coriander
1½ tsp ground cumin
½ tsp paprika
½ tsp ground cardamom
1 tbsp tomato purée
400ml water
100g peanut butter
salt and cayenne pepper

Heat the oil in a pan on a medium heat and fry the onion for 10 minutes, until lightly browned. Add the garlic, ginger and chilli and cook for a couple of minutes, stirring all the time. Add all the spices and cook for 30 seconds, until fragrant, then add the tomato purée and the water and simmer for 5 minutes.

Finally, add the peanut butter and stir until the mixture is smooth. Simmer for 5 minutes. The sauce should be thick but pourable. Add a little more water if needed.

Taste and add salt and a pinch of cayenne pepper if needed. Serve as a dip with naan bread or as a sauce over roasted sweet potatoes or rice.

BABA GANOUSH

You'll find versions of this dip all over the Middle East. My Mum taught me this recipe when I was 15 years old and I've made it ever since. It has a lovely smoky flavour and – once the aubergine is cooked – takes no time at all. *Pictured opposite (below), with Hummus (top; see page 46).*

SERVES 4

1 large or 2 medium
   aubergines, about 550g
3 tbsp tahini
2 tbsp warm water
1 garlic clove, finely chopped
1 tbsp white wine vinegar
pinch of cayenne pepper,
   plus extra to serve
1 tbsp chopped fresh parsley
salt

Preheat the oven to 220°C. Place the aubergine in a baking dish and roast for 40 minutes, or until well charred and soft. Set aside to cool.

When the aubergine is cool enough to handle, flake off the skin and place the flesh in a bowl. Using a fork, beat the aubergine until it forms a smooth purée.

Spoon the tahini into a separate bowl. Dilute with a tablespoon of the warm water; at first it will thicken. Add the remaining tablespoon of water and mix until the tahini becomes creamy again. Add the garlic, vinegar and aubergine purée and mix until well blended. Season with salt and cayenne pepper, then gently mix in the parsley.

Spoon into a serving bowl and sprinkle with a little more cayenne pepper to serve.

LUNCHES
AND DINNERS

BEEF & AUBERGINE CASSEROLE

Tepsi translates as 'casserole' and this is a traditional Persian dish of meatballs in tomato sauce with aubergine. It's quite rich. You could make it with less oil, I suppose, but then it wouldn't be so traditional – or taste so good.

SERVES 4-6

350g minced beef
4 large garlic cloves, crushed
¾ tsp curry powder
2 aubergines, about 700g,
    cut into 1.5cm slices
120ml olive oil
2 large potatoes, about 500g,
    peeled and cut into
    1.5cm slices
1 large onion, cut into
    1cm slices
1 large green pepper, cored,
    de-seeded and sliced
350ml water
4 tbsp tomato purée
1½ tbsp tamarind paste
1½ tbsp granulated sugar
3 tomatoes, about 280g, cut
    into 1cm slices
salt and white pepper
basmati rice or bread,
    to serve

Preheat the oven to 180°C.

Place the beef and two crushed garlic cloves in a bowl. Add the curry powder and some salt and pepper and mix by hand until well combined. Divide the mixture into 12 equal pieces and roll into balls. Set aside.

Heat a large non-stick frying pan on a medium–high heat. Brush both sides of the aubergine slices with olive oil and fry in batches for 4–5 minutes on each side, until golden. Set aside.

Brush the potato slices with oil and cook in the same pan for about 6 minutes on each side until golden but not completely cooked through. Set aside.

In the same pan, fry the onion slices and green pepper in about 2 tablespoons of the oil for about 5 minutes, until just golden. Add the remaining garlic and fry for 1 more minute. Set aside.

Finally, fry the meatballs on a high heat for 2–3 minutes until well browned but not cooked through.

In a measuring jug, mix the water with the tomato purée, tamarind paste and sugar until well blended.

Arrange half of the aubergine, potato, onion, pepper, tomatoes and meatballs in a 30cm round baking dish, overlapping them. Season well, then pour half of the tomato sauce over the top. Repeat with the rest of the vegetables and meatballs. Season well and pour the remaining sauce on top.

Cover with foil or a lid and bake for 30 minutes, then uncover and bake for another 20 minutes. Serve with basmati rice or bread to mop up the sauce.

SPICED LAMB PILAO

Many cultures have their own version of this dish and mine has Asian and Arab influences. But the thing to know about pilao is that you have to make it your own. It's trial and error, really. Just play around, adding your favourite spices – this recipe is how my family likes it, so you can use it as your starting point.

SERVES 4-6

4 tbsp sunflower oil

2 large onions, finely
    chopped

900g boneless lamb
    shoulder, cut into chunks

2 tbsp ginger paste

2 tbsp garlic paste

2 tbsp cumin seeds

8 whole cardamom pods,
    crushed

6 cloves

4 cinnamon sticks

550ml water

350g basmati rice

salt and pepper

For the minted yoghurt

150g natural yoghurt

small handful of fresh mint
    leaves, shredded

Heat 2 tablespoons of the oil in a large heavy-based pan on a medium heat. Add the onions and fry for 10 minutes until soft and golden.

Remove the onions from the pan and set aside. Add the remaining oil, then fry the lamb, in batches, until browned. Return all the browned lamb to the pan, along with the cooked onions, ginger paste, garlic paste, cumin seeds, crushed cardamom pods, cloves, cinnamon sticks and a pinch of salt and pepper. Mix well to combine. Add 400ml of the water and bring to the boil. Reduce the heat to a gentle simmer, cover with a tight-fitting lid and cook on a low heat for 3 hours, stirring occasionally. Add a little water if you find that it is drying out.

Once the lamb is very tender, add the rice and the remaining water, stir and bring to the boil. Reduce the heat, cover with the lid and cook for 15 minutes without removing the lid. Remove the pan from the heat, keeping the lid firmly on, and set aside for 15 minutes.

Meanwhile, combine the yoghurt with the mint leaves.

Remove the lid and use a large fork to fluff up the rice. Taste and adjust the seasoning if needed and serve with the minted yoghurt.

SANNA MIRZA'S *Ghormeh Sabzi*

PERSIAN LAMB & HERB STEW

My family are originally from Pakistan and my husband is from Iran. When I looked into it, I found connections between the Pakistani and Persian cultures going way back, which I try to bring into my recipes. This dish is my husband's favourite, so naturally it was the first one I learned to cook after we got married.

SERVES 4

5 tbsp vegetable oil

1 onion, finely chopped

4 garlic cloves, finely chopped

1 tsp ground turmeric

500g boneless lamb shoulder, cut into 2cm cubes

600ml water

4 Persian dried limes (available in Middle Eastern shops or online), each pierced with a knife

100g fresh flat-leaf parsley

75g fresh coriander

75g fresh chives

50g fresh fenugreek leaves (often sold as *methi*; substitute 1 tbsp dried fenugreek leaves if you can't find fresh)

1 tsp tomato purée

1 x 400g tin red kidney beans, drained and rinsed

salt and pepper

white rice and Salad Shirazi (see page 95), to serve

Heat 2 tablespoons of the oil in a large pan and fry the onion and garlic on a medium–high heat for 10 minutes, until golden. Add the turmeric and stir for 30 seconds until the onions are well coated. Add the meat, season with salt and pepper and fry for about 10 minutes, until browned.

Add the water and the dried limes. Bring to the boil and skim off any foam on the surface. Lower the heat, cover and simmer for 1½ hours.

While the meat is cooking, wash, dry and chop the herbs.

Heat the remaining oil in a large frying pan and stir-fry the herbs for 5–7 minutes, until wilted. Add the herbs and tomato purée to the meat, partly cover and let simmer for 30 minutes. Then add the beans and simmer, partly covered, for a final 30 minutes.

Taste and adjust the seasoning if needed, remove and discard the dried limes and serve with plain white rice and Salad Shirazi.

IRAQI DOLMA

I wasn't taught to cook, it was just what we did at home in Baghdad with my Mum and mother-in-law. You knew you'd got it right when guests asked for the recipes. This is a colourful dish – colour is important in Iraqi cooking. The pomegranate molasses and *baharat* spice (see page 34) are what gives it the Persian flavour.

SERVES 4-6

4 onions, peeled

280g basmati rice, rinsed
    and soaked in cold water
    for 30 minutes, then
    drained

280g minced lamb

3 tomatoes, chopped

2 garlic cloves, finely
    chopped

3 tbsp tamarind paste

3 tbsp pomegranate
    molasses

6 tbsp tomato purée

8 tbsp olive oil

2 tsp *baharat* (Lebanese
    seven-spice mix; see
    page 34)

2 tsp salt

4 long green peppers or
    romano peppers, cored
    and de-seeded

20 large vine leaves
    (preserved in brine),
    soaked in boiling water
    for 20 minutes, then
    drained and refreshed
    under cold water

600ml water

Make an incision in the onions from top to bottom on one side, cutting halfway through, stopping at the core. Bring a pan of water to the boil, add the onions and simmer for 12 minutes. Drain and rinse under cold water. When cool, separate each onion to make two or three shells (each shell should have two layers) and a small core. You need eight shells in total. Chop the onion cores and set aside.

Place the rice in a mixing bowl. Add the lamb, chopped onion, tomatoes and garlic, 1½ tablespoons of the tamarind paste, 1½ tablespoons of the pomegranate molasses, 3 tablespoons of the tomato purée, 4 tablespoons of the olive oil, the spice mix and 1½ teaspoons of the salt. Mix delicately with your hands until well blended, taking care not to break up the rice too much.

Make an incision in the peppers from top to bottom and fill with some of the rice mixture; don't pack too tightly, as the rice expands as it cooks. Fill the onion shells likewise.

Place 1 heaped tablespoon of the rice mixture in the centre of each vine leaf, near the stem. Fold the stem end over the filling, fold in both sides and roll up loosely to allow space for the rice to expand.

Snugly fit all the stuffed vegetables and leaves in a large deep pan with a tight-fitting lid. Mix the remaining tamarind paste, pomegranate molasses, tomato purée, olive oil and salt with the water, then pour over the dolma. Invert a large plate on top to hold everything in place. Cover with the lid, bring to the boil, then simmer on a low heat for 45 minutes–1 hour, or until the rice is cooked and most of the liquid has been absorbed.

Remove the lid and plate, place a large serving platter over the pan and carefully flip the contents onto the platter. *Pictured overleaf.*

GREEN RICE

I have a master's degree in chemistry, but when I came to Britain from Iraq it wasn't easy to combine that with family life, so now the kitchen is my laboratory. With the mixing, pouring and measuring, I feel like I am back in my old world. This is a version of a traditional dish, which I made up. It's a good centrepiece because the colour is so striking.

SERVES 4

500g lamb neck fillet or
    boneless lamb shoulder,
    cut into 3cm cubes
1 litre chicken stock (made
    with 2 stock cubes)
300g basmati rice
250g frozen broad beans
4 tbsp sunflower oil
2 garlic cloves, crushed
40g fresh dill, finely chopped
2 tbsp dried dill

For the cucumber, dill and
    yoghurt sauce
1 cucumber, coarsely grated
500g full-fat natural yoghurt
1 tsp dried dill
1 tbsp olive oil
salt and pepper

Place the lamb and stock in a large pan and bring to the boil. Skim off the foam on the surface, reduce the heat to medium–low and gently simmer for 1 hour (or 1½ hours if you are using lamb shoulder), until cooked through.

Wash the rice and leave to soak for 30 minutes. Blanch the broad beans in a pan of boiling water for 2–3 minutes, drain and refresh under cold water. Remove the outer skins.

When the lamb is cooked, drain and reserve the stock. Heat half of the oil in a heavy-based pan and fry the garlic until it just starts to colour. Add the cooked lamb and fry for 5–6 minutes until evenly browned, stirring all the time. Add the broad beans and half of the fresh and dried dill and cook for 2 minutes. Transfer to a plate, set aside and keep warm.

In the same pan, heat the remaining oil on a low–medium heat. Drain the rice and add to the pan, stirring until all the grains are coated with oil. Add 500ml of the meat stock, bring to a simmer, cover with a tight-fitting lid, then turn the heat to the lowest setting and cook for 30 minutes.

Meanwhile, make the yoghurt sauce. Mix the grated cucumber and yoghurt in a bowl. Season to taste. Sprinkle with the dried dill and drizzle with the olive oil.

When the rice is ready, stir it with a fork to fluff it. Add the rest of the fresh and dried dill, the reserved meat and broad beans, and stir gently. Add a little of the reserved stock if you need extra moisture and cook on a low heat for about 8 minutes. Serve immediately, with the cucumber, dill and yoghurt sauce.

PERSIAN CHICKEN WITH BARBERRY RICE

This recipe is a favourite of mine and always seems to please guests at the dinner table. The jewelled rice gives it a sweet, tangy, mouth-watering taste and, although the dish takes a bit of time, it's pretty easy to make. It's worth it because the end result is so spectacular.

SERVES 4-6

For the chicken

2 small ice cubes

generous pinch of saffron
  threads, ground to
  a powder

25g butter

8 bone-in skinless chicken
  thighs (or buy with skin
  on, pull off the skin
  and discard)

2 onions: 1 quartered,
  1 thinly sliced

1 tsp ground turmeric

1 tsp salt

1 tsp freshly ground
  black pepper

700ml water

2 tbsp ghee or vegetable oil

2 tbsp tomato purée

2 tbsp freshly squeezed
  lemon juice

1 tbsp dried barberries,
  rinsed

Continued overleaf

For the chicken: Place the ice cubes in a small bowl, sprinkle the crushed saffron over the top and set aside. As the ice melts, the saffron will slowly release its bright orange colour and pungent flavour.

Melt the butter in a sauté pan on a medium heat and fry the chicken pieces for 5 minutes on each side, until lightly golden. Add the onion quarters, sprinkle with the turmeric, salt and pepper and cover with the water. Bring to the boil and skim off any foam on the surface. Lower the heat, cover and simmer for 15 minutes. Turn the thighs and simmer, covered, for another 15 minutes.

Meanwhile, in a separate pan, fry the sliced onion in the ghee or vegetable oil for 10–15 minutes, until golden brown. Add the tomato purée and stir for a minute to coat the onion. Set aside.

Remove about half of the stock and the onion quarters from the chicken pan. Reserve the stock for later (save the onions for a soup or a stew).

Pour the saffron water over the chicken. Add the fried onion and tomato purée mixture, the lemon juice and barberries and stir well. Cover and simmer for another 15 minutes.

(This is a good point to start making the barberry rice, see overleaf.)

Turn the chicken thighs again and simmer, covered, for a final 15 minutes. The sauce should be well reduced and glossy. If the sauce is too thin, remove the chicken and boil to reduce until thick; if it is too thick, add some of the reserved stock. Keep warm while you finish the rice.

Continued overleaf

For the barberry rice

2 litres water

400g basmati rice

½ tsp ground cinnamon

½ tsp dried crushed edible
   rose petals

¼ tsp ground cumin

⅛ tsp ground cardamom

1 tbsp salt

5 tbsp ghee or vegetable oil

1 onion, finely chopped

25g dried barberries,
   rinsed and soaked
   for 15 minutes

chopped almonds and/or
   pistachios, to garnish

For the barberry rice: In a large heavy-based pan (covered with a tight-fitting lid), bring the water to the boil.

Put the rice in a bowl and wash several times under running water, stirring gently with your fingers. When the water is clear, drain the rice.

Mix the cinnamon, rose petals, cumin and cardamom until well blended. Set aside.

Add the salt to the boiling water, then add the rice. Let the water come back to the boil, stir the rice and cook, uncovered, for about 7 minutes. It should be soft on the outside and slightly hard inside.

Drain the rice. Return the pan to the heat and add 3 tablespoons of the ghee or vegetable oil. Spoon half of the rice into the pan, then sprinkle with half of the spice mixture. Spoon the remaining rice on top and sprinkle with the remaining spices. Poke the handle of the spoon into the rice, making five holes to let the steam escape. Wrap the lid in a clean tea towel and place on top of the pan. Turn the heat to low and cook for 30 minutes.

For the rice garnish, heat the remaining 2 tablespoons of ghee or vegetable oil in a small frying pan on a medium heat and fry the onion for 10 minutes, until golden. Drain the barberries and squeeze out the excess water. Add them to the onion and stir for 30 seconds, taking care as the barberries tend to burn easily.

When ready to serve, stir the rice gently with a fork to mix the spices evenly, and spoon onto a serving plate. Garnish with the onion and barberry mixture and sprinkle chopped almonds and/or pistachios over the top. Serve with the chicken.

FAIZA HAYANI BELLILI'S

ALGERIAN COUSCOUS

I used to run my own translation agency in Algeria. When I moved to London I very much missed my work and was initially very lonely. So, while my children napped, I cooked. Cooking became an important connection to home for me. It eventually led me here to the Community Kitchen, where I made great friends. This is a traditional Algerian dish (we use any veg we have to hand), which includes the proper way to cook couscous.

SERVES 4

3 tbsp olive oil

1 onion, chopped

1 large garlic clove, minced

1 chicken, about 1.6kg,
    jointed into 8 pieces

1 heaped tsp ras-el-hanout
    spice mix

1 large carrot, peeled and cut
    into 4 chunks

1 large waxy potato, peeled
    and quartered

150g swede, peeled and cut
    into 3cm chunks

1 large celery stick, cut into 4

800ml water

2 tsp salt

½ tsp ground black pepper

1 mild green chilli

1 large courgette, cut into 4

1 large parsnip, peeled,
    quartered, core removed

½ x 400g tin chopped
    tomatoes

100g tinned chickpeas,
    drained and rinsed

¼ tsp dried mint

300g couscous (any type)

120ml warm water

2 tbsp ghee or butter, melted

Heat the oil in a large frying pan, add the onion, garlic and chicken pieces and cook on a medium–high heat for 6–7 minutes until golden. Add the ras-el-hanout and stir until the ingredients are well coated with the spice mix. Transfer to a couscous pot or a heavy-based pan with a lid. Add the carrot, potato, swede, celery and water and bring to the boil. Skim off the foam, add 1½ teaspoons of the salt, the pepper and the whole green chilli. Lower the heat, cover with the lid and simmer for 40 minutes.

Add the courgette, parsnip, tomatoes, chickpeas, mint and a little more water if needed. Simmer, covered, for 30 minutes.

Spread the couscous in a large shallow dish. Dissolve the remaining salt in the warm water. Sprinkle the salted water over the grains and mix with your hands until all the grains are wet. Set aside for 5 minutes. Break up the couscous with your fingers, rolling some of it between your palms to separate and aerate the grains.

If you are using a couscous pot, line the top with cheesecloth, add the couscous and cover with the lid. Alternatively, fit a colander over a pan of boiling water, add the couscous and cover tightly with foil to prevent the steam escaping. Steam the couscous for 12 minutes.

Transfer back into the dish and, when cool enough to handle, mix the couscous by hand, as before, to separate and aerate the grains. Repeat the steaming and mixing twice. When the couscous is ready, drizzle the ghee or butter over the top and mix delicately, using two forks, until all the ghee is incorporated.

Spoon the couscous onto plates. Add some chicken and vegetables and ladle the sauce on top. Serve any extra sauce on the side.

AYSHA BORA'S *Kuku Paka*

COCONUT CHICKEN CURRY

✳✳✳ When I was growing up I hated cooking. My family is from India and preparing big meals
✳✳✳ for the extended family was part of our culture, but I used to beg for any job other than
cooking. Then I got married and moved to Africa and suddenly everything changed – I began
calling my mother and asking her for recipes. She told me: 'Cooking for someone you love is
what makes you a good cook.' This curry is a particular favourite of my family in Tanzania.

SERVES 4

1 large chicken, jointed into
   8 pieces, excess skin
   trimmed away
1 large ripe tomato,
   roughly chopped
1 onion, quartered
15g fresh root ginger, peeled
4 garlic cloves, peeled
6 serrano chillies, stems
   removed and de-seeded
   (use fewer if you prefer
   milder curries)
2 tsp ground cumin
1 tsp ground coriander
1 tsp ground turmeric
2 tbsp coconut oil
2 x 400ml tins coconut milk
3 eggs, hard-boiled, peeled
   and halved
juice of ½ lemon
salt and pepper
10g fresh coriander,
   chopped, to garnish
rice, chapatis or flatbreads,
   to serve

Score each piece of the chicken in two or three places, slicing about
1cm into the meat.

Put the tomato, onion, ginger, garlic, chillies, cumin, coriander,
turmeric and some salt and pepper into a food processor and blend
to a rough paste. Rub one third of the paste all over the chicken,
into the cuts and under the skin; reserve the rest of the mixture.
Refrigerate the chicken for at least 1 hour, or up to 5 hours.

Preheat the grill to the highest setting, and line a large baking tin
with foil.

In a large pan, melt the coconut oil on a medium heat; add the
remaining paste and cook, stirring occasionally, for 20 minutes
or until all of the moisture evaporates. Increase the heat slightly
and cook for 3–5 minutes until the paste is thick and dark. Add
the coconut milk and simmer for 25–30 minutes until the sauce
is thick.

Meanwhile, put the marinated chicken, skin side up, in the lined
baking tin and grill for 15 minutes, until well coloured and charred,
then turn the chicken over and grill for another 5 minutes to make
sure it is cooked through.

Stir the chicken and any juices into the curry pan, bring to a simmer,
cover and cook for 5 minutes until the flavours have combined.
Taste and adjust the seasoning if necessary. Add the boiled eggs
and the lemon juice to taste. Sprinkle with the chopped coriander
and serve with rice, chapatis or flatbreads.

AMAAL ABD ELRASOUL'S

CHICKEN & MUSHROOM CREAM SOUP

I live in Cairo, but came over after the Grenfell fire to help my sister-in-law Munira. I got this recipe from a neighbour back home. It is very special – shredded chicken in a creamy base scented with cardamom, cinnamon and ginger – so naturally I made it for the women in the Kitchen. I guarantee you won't have had chicken soup like this before.

SERVES 4

60g butter
2 onions, chopped
2 garlic cloves, finely sliced
5 cardamom pods,
   lightly crushed
2 cloves
2 bay leaves
½ tsp ground ginger
¼ tsp ground allspice
pinch of ground cinnamon
½ chicken, about 650g
1 litre water
3 tbsp plain flour
150ml double cream
250g mushrooms, sliced
fresh flat-leaf parsley,
   to garnish

Melt 20g of the butter in a large heavy-based saucepan on a low–medium heat. Add the onions and cook for 5 minutes, until soft.

Add the garlic and spices and cook for a minute, until fragrant. Add the chicken, skin side down, and the water. Bring to a simmer, skim off the foam on the surface and cook for 35 minutes. Turn off the heat and leave to cool for about an hour.

When the chicken is cool enough to handle, strain the stock and reserve. Peel off and discard the chicken skin. Shred the chicken into bite-sized pieces and set aside.

Melt 25g of the butter in the pan used for the stock. Stir in the flour and cook for a minute, until the paste is lightly golden. Whisk in the reserved stock and the cream and bring to a simmer.

Meanwhile, melt the remaining butter in a frying pan on a medium heat and stir-fry the mushrooms for 5 minutes, until lightly golden and the liquid has evaporated.

Add the mushrooms and shredded chicken to the soup and simmer for 10–15 minutes. Serve garnished with the parsley.

JEERA CHICKEN

I was born and raised in west London but am ethnically Indian. When I was growing up, cooking was one of the ways I bonded with my mother – Mama Jay. My goal was always to make a dish so that my father and brothers assumed she had made it. This is one of her favourites. Cooked in plenty of yoghurt with aromatic cumin, the curry is quick and easy to prepare and makes a delicious supper for all the family.

SERVES 4

2 tbsp cumin seeds

2 tbsp sunflower oil

2 red onions, thinly sliced

25g fresh root ginger, peeled
    and grated

40g green chillies, de-seeded
    and sliced

2 tsp ground turmeric

1 tsp sea salt

8 bone-in skinless chicken
    thighs (or buy with skin
    on, pull off the skin
    and discard)

300–500g natural yoghurt,
    at room temperature

1½ tbsp garam masala

juice of ½ lemon

15g fresh coriander,
    chopped

salt and pepper

rice and/or pittas or
    flatbreads, to serve

Heat a large pan on a low–medium heat, add the cumin seeds and gently toast until fragrant, then transfer to a bowl and set aside. Add the oil to the pan and when it is hot, add the onions and let them gently sizzle for 10 minutes until soft and golden.

Add the toasted cumin seeds, ginger and chillies to the pan and fry for a minute, then add the turmeric and salt and stir to combine. Increase the heat slightly, add the chicken, and cook for about 5 minutes, then reduce the heat slightly and add 300g yoghurt to the pan, adding more as necessary to ensure the chicken is submerged in the sauce. Gently simmer, stirring often, for 30–35 minutes until the chicken is cooked through: the yoghurt will split at first, but will come back together and form a creamy sauce.

Add the garam masala, lemon juice and coriander and stir to combine. Taste, season if needed and serve immediately, with rice and/or pittas or flatbreads.

BAKED FISH WITH TAHINI & POMEGRANATE

This is a recipe from my Algerian Dad – and it's so easy I'm almost embarrassed to call it a recipe! It works well with all kinds of fish, even salmon, and it's a great way of using up any tahini you have left over after you've made hummus.

SERVES 4

4 skinless boneless fillets of
  cod or other fish, about
  150g each
1 tbsp olive oil
4 tbsp tahini
juice of 1 lemon
1 garlic clove, grated
2–4 tbsp warm water
10g fresh flat-leaf parsley,
  roughly torn
50g fresh pomegranate seeds
50g pine nuts, toasted
  (see page 127)
salt and pepper

Preheat the oven to 180°C. Place the fish in a baking dish and drizzle with the oil, season with salt and pepper, then bake for 10–12 minutes, depending on the thickness of your fish.

In a bowl, mix the tahini, lemon juice, garlic and some salt and pepper. Gradually add the warm water until you reach the consistency of natural yoghurt.

In another bowl, mix the parsley, pomegranate seeds and pine nuts. This is your garnish.

When the fish is cooked, plate and pour over the sauce. Sprinkle over the garnish to serve.

TUNA, OLIVE & SUN-DRIED TOMATO CAKE

This is so easy and quick – it has become my emergency dish! I keep all the simple storecupboard ingredients on hand so I can make it any time. You can serve it hot or cold and it's perfect for picnics.

SERVES 4-6

150g plain flour

1 tsp baking powder

1 tsp ground turmeric

1 tsp ground cumin

3 eggs

2 x 160g tins tuna in sunflower oil

100g pitted mixed olives, roughly chopped

40g sun-dried tomatoes in oil, drained and chopped

100g Cheddar cheese, grated

Preheat the oven to 180°C. Line a 1kg loaf tin with baking paper.

Place the flour, baking powder and spices in a large mixing bowl and stir with a whisk until well blended.

Make a hollow in the centre and crack in the eggs. Start mixing from the centre, gradually combining the flour with the eggs until just blended. Add the tuna and its oil, the olives, sun-dried tomatoes and cheese and gently fold together with a spatula.

Pour the mixture into the prepared tin. Bake for 35–40 minutes, until lightly golden on top and springy to the touch. Leave to cool in the tin for 5–10 minutes before turning out. Serve hot or cold, sliced.

AUBERGINE MASALA

It was 1976 and our mother was teaching me and my teenage sisters to cook – passing on her recipes. I was the best at making aubergine masala, so she allowed me to call it my signature dish – I've made it ever since. Back home in Uganda, I run a restaurant where I serve this along with other local dishes. When I'm in London helping my daughter Munira with my grandchildren, I make it for them and for the women at the Community Kitchen.

SERVES 4

4 tbsp sunflower oil

2 large aubergines, chopped into 4cm cubes

350g new potatoes, halved

2 tsp cumin seeds

1 tsp mustard seeds

1 tsp fenugreek seeds

1 large onion, finely chopped

3 dried curry leaves

3 tbsp tomato purée

1 tbsp garlic paste

1 tbsp ginger paste

1 tsp ground turmeric

4 vine tomatoes, finely chopped

200ml water

3 tbsp chopped fresh coriander

For the rice

600ml water

pinch of salt

300g basmati rice

Heat 2 tablespoons of the oil in a large frying pan on a high heat. Add the aubergines and fry, stirring often, for 10 minutes or until well browned. Tip the aubergines into a large bowl and set aside. Reduce the heat to medium–high and add 1 tablespoon of the oil to the pan. Add the potatoes and fry, stirring often, for 10 minutes or until golden brown. Add the fried potatoes to the aubergines and set aside.

Heat a large pan on a medium–high heat, add the cumin, mustard and fenugreek seeds and toast until fragrant, 2–3 minutes. Then add the remaining oil and, when it is hot, add the onion and curry leaves and fry for 10 minutes until soft and golden.

Add the tomato purée and cook for 2 minutes, then add the garlic paste, ginger paste, turmeric and tomatoes. Cook for about 5 minutes, until the tomato juice has evaporated and the mixture is starting to dry out in the pan.

Meanwhile, prepare the rice. Put the water and salt in a pan and bring to the boil. Add the rice, reduce the heat slightly, cover and boil for 10 minutes. Remove the pan from the heat, keeping the lid firmly on, and set aside for 10 minutes.

Add the fried aubergines and potatoes to the curry pan, along with the water. Bring to the boil, then reduce the heat to a simmer, cover and cook for 15 minutes, stirring occasionally. Remove the lid and simmer for 5–10 minutes or until the vegetables are tender. Add half the chopped coriander and stir through.

Remove the lid from the rice and fluff up with a fork. Serve alongside the curry, sprinkled with the remaining coriander.

ETHIOPIAN SPICY RED LENTILS & GREENS WITH TOMATO SALAD

Grenfell was such a great community, so it's really nice to come along to the Hubb Kitchen and be back among the people who were your neighbours; it's a real social gathering. My recipes are from Ethiopia, where I lived until I was 12. They are vegan, although you really don't miss the meat. My family isn't vegetarian, but we do like to have some meat-free meals. And if you are cooking for a crowd with many different backgrounds, as we are here, then it's good to have something everyone can eat.

Ethiopian meals are traditionally served on a large spongy flatbread called *injera*. It's tricky to make, but you can source it online (try tobiateff.co.uk) or at your local Ethiopian restaurant. Stews and salads are heaped directly onto the *injera*, which you tear with your fingers and use to scoop up each flavoursome mouthful. Rice or bread are perfectly fine accompaniments too.

SERVES 4

For the berbere *spice mix*
2 tbsp paprika
2 tsp ground coriander
1 tsp cayenne pepper
½ tsp freshly ground black
    pepper
½ tsp ground fenugreek
½ tsp ground allspice
½ tsp ground ginger
½ ground cinnamon
¼ tsp ground cardamom
¼ tsp ground cloves
¼ tsp ground nutmeg
1 tsp salt

For the misir wot *(lentils)*
4 tbsp vegetable oil
1½ onions, about 175g,
    finely chopped

For the berbere *spice mix*: Mix all the spices and the salt until well blended. This makes more than you need for this recipe. It will keep for up to 6 months in an airtight container.

For the misir wot *(lentils)*: Heat the oil in a heavy-based pan on a medium heat and fry the onions for 5 minutes, until soft.

Add the ginger and garlic and fry for 5 minutes, until lightly browned. Add 1 tablespoon of the *berbere* spice mix and fry for 1 minute, until fragrant. Add the tomato purée and fry for a minute, stirring until the onions are well coated.

Add the lentils and water and simmer for 25–40 minutes (depending on the brand of lentil you use), until all the water has been absorbed and the lentils are soft. Taste and season if needed.

While the lentils are cooking you can prepare the *gomen wot* and tomato salad.

Continued overleaf

Continued overleaf

1 tbsp grated fresh root
ginger, about 20g
3 garlic cloves, crushed
1 tbsp *berbere* spice mix
(see page 83)
3 tbsp tomato purée
200g red lentils, rinsed
600ml water
salt

For the gomen wot (*greens*)
4 tbsp vegetable oil
1 onion, very finely chopped
2 tbsp grated fresh root
ginger, about 40g
6 garlic cloves, crushed
½ tsp ground turmeric
500g frozen whole leaf
spinach
salt and pepper

For the tomato salad
3 tomatoes, chopped
½ red onion, finely chopped
1 jalapeño pepper,
de-seeded and
finely chopped
juice of ½ lemon
2 tbsp rice vinegar
½ tsp salt
⅛ tsp ground black pepper
1 tsp caster sugar, or to taste
2 tbsp olive oil

injera, baguette, pittas or rice,
to serve

For the gomen wot (*greens*): Heat the oil in a pan on a medium heat and fry the onion for 5 minutes, until soft. Add the ginger and garlic and fry for a further 5 minutes, stirring constantly, until lightly golden. Add the turmeric and fry for 30 seconds, stirring to coat the onion. Add the frozen spinach, cover and cook for 15–20 minutes, or until the spinach is fully cooked. Season with salt and pepper to taste.

For the tomato salad: Combine the tomatoes, onion and jalapeño in a bowl.

Place the lemon juice, vinegar, salt, pepper and sugar in a separate bowl and stir until the salt and sugar have dissolved. Whisk in the oil until well blended. Pour the dressing over the tomatoes and leave to infuse for 10 minutes.

To finish: Serve the *misir wot*, *gomen wot* and salad to the table in separate bowls, accompanied by *injera*, baguette, pittas or rice.

LEBANESE VEGETABLE LASAGNE

My mother was Irish, my father Algerian; I was raised in France and went to school in Switzerland, so I had a real melting pot of influences, but I definitely got my love of cooking from my father's side. In Middle Eastern culture, cooking is a show of love – and that's what we do here at the Kitchen. This vegetarian lasagne is something I developed for my kids to get them to eat more veggies. They even prefer it to the meat version.

SERVES 4

5 tbsp olive oil, plus extra
    for greasing
1 aubergine, cut into
    1.5cm chunks
2 red peppers, cored,
    de-seeded and cut into
    1.5cm chunks
1 courgette, cut into
    1.5cm chunks
1 red onion, cut into
    1.5cm chunks
2 large tomatoes, chopped
2 tbsp ground coriander
½ tsp chilli flakes, or to taste
100g fresh spinach
2 tbsp boiling water
10 dried lasagne sheets
350g natural yoghurt
2 eggs
3 tbsp tahini
200g feta cheese, crumbled
200g mozzarella,
    finely chopped
salt and pepper
lemon wedges, to serve

Preheat the oven to 180°C. Grease a 30 x 20 x 5cm baking dish.

Heat 2 tablespoons of the oil in a large frying pan on a medium–high heat and fry the aubergine for 10–12 minutes, until soft and golden. Season with salt and pepper and set aside.

Add a tablespoon of oil to the pan and fry the peppers and courgette for 7–8 minutes, until soft and lightly brown. Season and set aside.

Add the remaining oil to the pan and fry the onion for 5 minutes, until soft and lightly caramelised. Add the tomatoes and fry for 2 minutes, until just soft but still holding their shape. Season, add the coriander and chilli flakes and cook until fragrant. Add the reserved aubergine, peppers and courgette, stir to combine, then set aside.

Cook the spinach in the 2 tablespoons of boiling water for 30 seconds, until just wilted. Drain and, when cold enough to handle, squeeze dry. Add to the vegetable mixture.

Cook the lasagne sheets in a pan of simmering water, in batches, for 4–5 minutes, until pliable but not fully cooked.

In a bowl, whisk together the yoghurt, eggs and tahini. Season well.

Spread a third of the cooked vegetables in the baking dish. Top with three lasagne sheets. Spread a third of the yoghurt mixture on top, then scatter over a third of both the feta and mozzarella. Repeat the layers twice, using four lasagne sheets for the final layer. Season well, then place the dish on a baking sheet. Bake for 35–40 minutes, until golden and bubbling. Serve with lemon wedges.

MOROCCAN CHICKPEA & NOODLE SOUP

✱✱✱ When I was growing up, our neighbours were Moroccan and we were often invited to share a bowl of *harira* with them. Eventually I started making it for myself. I always use organic ingredients and it makes a delicious and substantial meal. We eat it with chopped dates – that doesn't sound like it should work, but it does! Make sure that all your stirring is done with love and prayer.

SERVES 4-6

2 onions, roughly chopped

4 celery sticks, chopped

1 x 400g tin chopped
  tomatoes

25g fresh coriander

20g fresh parsley

1 tsp ground black pepper

½ tsp ground white pepper

½ tsp ground turmeric

1 cinnamon stick

1 tsp ground ginger

1½ tsp salt (see note)

½ tbsp olive oil

1 litre boiling water

½ x 400g tin chickpeas,
  drained, rinsed and loose
  skins removed

35g brown rice vermicelli
  noodles, crushed by hand

15g wholemeal flour

1 egg, beaten

½ tsp *smen* (see note)
  or 1 tsp ghee

handful of pitted dates,
  chopped, to garnish

bread, such as *Khobz* (page
  92), and lemon wedges
  (optional), to serve

Place the onions, celery, tomatoes, coriander and parsley in a food processor and process until smooth. Pour the puréed ingredients into a large pan. Add the spices, salt and olive oil and bring to the boil, then simmer for about 15 minutes, stirring occasionally.

Add the boiling water, turn up the heat and boil for 20–25 minutes, until the liquid has reduced and thickened.

Add the chickpeas and noodles, turn the heat to low and simmer for 5 minutes.

Mix the flour with 2–3 tablespoons of water to make a soft paste. Turn up the heat and when the mixture starts to boil, whisk the flour paste into the soup until well blended.

Whisk the egg into the soup along with the *smen* or ghee, whisking all the time. Turn the heat to the lowest setting and simmer for 5 minutes.

Serve the soup in bowls, garnished with chopped dates, with bread and, if you like, lemon wedges to squeeze in.

NOTES I like to use pink Himalayan salt, but you can use regular salt if you wish.

Smen is Moroccan fermented butter and can be found in Middle Eastern stores or online.

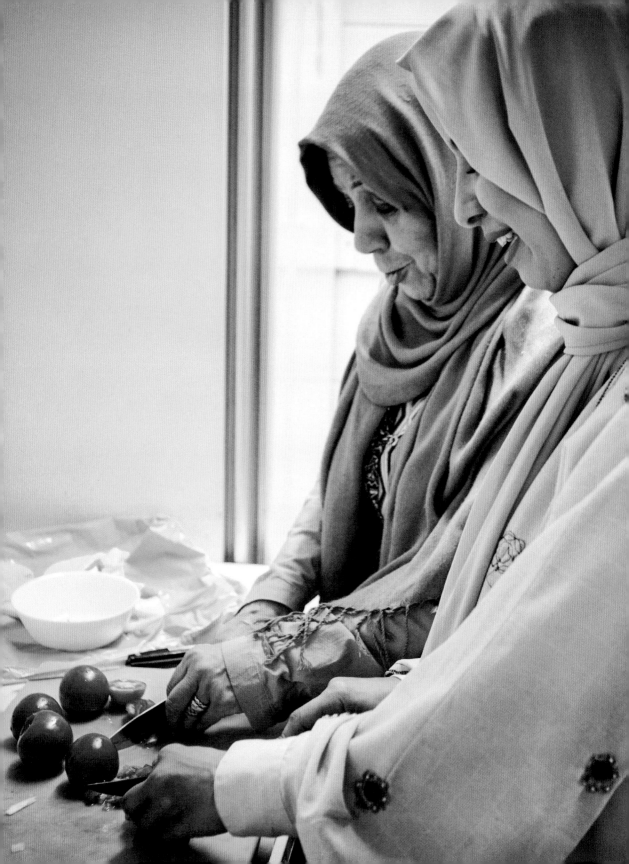

SALADS
AND
SIDES

FATTOUSH SALAD

Fattoush is a classic in Arab cooking. Sumac gives it authentic flavour and isn't hard to find. I came to the UK in 1989 and even back then it was easy to get all the ingredients I needed to cook recipes from home. Now, with the internet, you can order anything you need online.

**SERVES 4 AS A MAIN
OR 6 AS A SIDE**

2 pitta breads

7 tbsp extra-virgin olive oil

3 ripe tomatoes, quartered
and cut into 1cm slices

1 small cucumber, about
175g, halved lengthways
and cut into 1cm slices

½ green pepper, cored,
de-seeded and
finely chopped

150g radishes, trimmed
and quartered

2 baby gem lettuces, cored
and roughly chopped

3 spring onions,
finely chopped

3 tbsp finely chopped fresh
parsley (optional)

1 tbsp finely chopped
fresh mint

juice of ½ lemon

2 tbsp pomegranate
molasses

good pinch of sumac
(optional; see note)

salt and pepper

Preheat the oven to 180°C. Line a baking sheet with baking paper.

Split the pittas in half horizontally, then tear each half into 2cm pieces. Place in a bowl, add 2 tablespoons of the olive oil and salt and pepper to taste; toss to combine. Spread on the prepared baking sheet and bake for about 10 minutes, until golden and crisp. Set aside.

Place the chopped vegetables in a salad bowl, add the spring onions and chopped herbs.

Add the lemon juice and pomegranate molasses, season with the salt and pepper and toss well. Drizzle with the remaining olive oil and toss again.

Top with the crispy pitta, sprinkle with sumac, if you like, and serve immediately.

NOTE Sumac is a spice with a red colour and a lemony flavour; it is sold in Middle Eastern food shops, large supermarkets and online.

YEMENI BREAD

The smell of this baking takes me back to our little village in Yemen. It's the traditional bread my Mum used to make when I was growing up. It's what my son calls 'gida cooking', which is Yemeni for 'grandma cooking'. You can eat it with butter or jam but back home we had it with olives and dipped in sesame oil.

SERVES 4-6

475g strong bread flour, plus extra for dusting

1 tsp salt

3.5g fast-action dried yeast (half of a 7g sachet)

275ml warm water

½ tbsp olive oil, plus extra for greasing

Put the flour and salt in a large mixing bowl. Mix to combine, then make a hollow in the centre. Add the yeast to the hollow with a splash of the warm water and mix with your fingertips to help dissolve the yeast. Once dissolved, continue to gradually add the water and combine all the ingredients to form a sticky dough. Cover the bowl with three clean tea towels and leave to rest in a warm place for 5 minutes.

Lightly oil two baking sheets. Turn the dough out onto a lightly floured surface and knead for 10 minutes, until smooth. Divide into three pieces (about 250g each), then knead each piece of dough for 1 minute and roll into a smooth ball. Transfer two balls to one oiled baking sheet, and the third to the second sheet. Cover with clean tea towels and leave to rest for 10 minutes.

Preheat the oven to 190°C.

Using your hands or a rolling pin, flatten each dough ball to form a 15cm disc, no more than 2cm thick. Cover and rest again for 15 minutes.

Brush each disc with the olive oil and prick four times with a fork. Transfer to the oven and bake for 10 minutes, then swap the baking sheets over so the bread colours evenly and bake for a final 10 minutes. Serve warm, with mint tea, butter and jam.

SALAD SHIRAZI

 This is a simple salad, with just a few ingredients, from the south of Iran. The fresh flavours go well with chicken, or with lamb dishes such as *Ghormeh Sabzi* (see page 57).

SERVES 4

3 small Persian cucumbers
    (see note), about 350g,
    de-seeded and diced
3 ripe tomatoes, about 300g,
    de-seeded and diced
¼ red onion, finely diced
grated zest and juice
    of 1 lime (see note)
¼ tsp salt
¼ tsp ground black pepper
2 tbsp olive oil

Mix the diced cucumber, tomato and onion in a serving bowl.

Add the lime zest and juice, salt, pepper and olive oil. Toss gently until all the ingredients are well coated and serve immediately.

NOTE Persian cucumbers are supposed to be less bitter, but it is fine to use regular ones. You can also use lemon zest and juice in place of the lime, if you wish.

COLESLAW

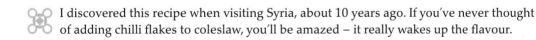 I discovered this recipe when visiting Syria, about 10 years ago. If you've never thought of adding chilli flakes to coleslaw, you'll be amazed – it really wakes up the flavour.

SERVES 4

2 carrots, peeled and
    coarsely grated
400g white cabbage, sliced
½ red pepper, cored, de-
    seeded and finely diced
25g fresh coriander, chopped
3 tbsp mayonnaise
7 tbsp natural yoghurt
¼ tsp ground black pepper
¼ tsp dried chilli flakes
salt

Place all the ingredients in a large serving bowl and toss well, with love and care, to combine. Taste and adjust the seasoning if necessary and chill in the fridge for at least 1 hour before serving.

TABBOULEH

 In Arab cooking, we always have pickles and olives on the table, and every meal needs something green. More often than not, it's tabbouleh.

SERVES 4

40g bulgur wheat

75ml boiling water

100g fresh parsley, chopped

10g fresh mint, stalks
   discarded and leaves
   finely chopped

2 spring onions, thinly sliced

⅓ cucumber, peeled,
   de-seeded and
   finely chopped

200g baby plum tomatoes:
   150g finely chopped,
   50g left whole

40g pitted green olives

For the dressing

4 tbsp olive oil

juice of 1½ lemons

2 tbsp pomegranate
   molasses

salt and pepper

Put the bulgur wheat in a small bowl, add the boiling water, then immediately cover tightly with foil and place a clean tea towel on top. Leave to steam for 20 minutes.

To make the dressing, mix the olive oil, lemon juice and pomegranate molasses with a pinch of salt and pepper.

Using a fork, fluff up the bulgur wheat (don't worry if there is a little liquid left), then add to a mixing bowl. Add the parsley, mint, spring onions, cucumber and chopped tomatoes and a pinch of salt and pepper. Mix to combine; taste and adjust the seasoning if necessary. Add half the dressing and mix well; taste and add the remaining dressing if you like.

Serve in a dish with the whole tomatoes and olives on top.

RAINBOW ROASTED VEGETABLES

To me, the way the table looks is as important as how the food tastes. I make sure there are always flowers on the tables at Al-Manaar. And I make this dish often because it adds beautiful colour to any meal.

SERVES 4-6

250g purple or waxy potatoes, scrubbed, cut into wedges

200g each beetroot and golden beetroot, peeled and cut into thin wedges

350g kabocha or butternut squash, de-seeded and cut into 2cm wedges

120g baby carrots, scrubbed, or regular carrots, peeled and cut into chunky strips

175g baby parsnips, scrubbed and halved, or regular parsnips, peeled and cut into chunky strips

4 tbsp extra-virgin olive oil

½ tsp dried chilli flakes

2 tsp dried oregano

2 small red and/or yellow peppers, de-seeded, cut into chunky strips or rings

1 courgette, sliced

150g Brussels sprouts, halved

1 watermelon radish, halved, sliced into half-moons, or 120g mooli, scrubbed and cut into 3cm slices

12 asparagus tips

salt and pepper

Preheat the oven to 200°C. You will need two large baking tins: the vegetables need to be baked separately because of their different cooking times.

Arrange the potatoes, beetroot, squash, carrots and parsnips in one of the tins, in a single layer. Drizzle with 1½ tablespoons of the olive oil, sprinkle with half the chilli flakes and oregano and season with salt and pepper. Bake on the top shelf of the oven for 20 minutes.

Arrange the rest of the vegetables in the second baking tin in a single layer, drizzle with the remaining olive oil, sprinkle with the remaining chilli flakes and oregano, and season.

When the first tin of vegetables has cooked for 20 minutes, move it to the middle shelf and place the second tin on the top shelf. Cook both tins for 15–20 minutes, or until all the vegetables are tender but not mushy.

Tip all the vegetables into a serving dish, taste and adjust the seasoning if necessary and then serve.

NOTE If you want the vegetables to be more charred, remove from the oven after 10–15 minutes and place each tin under a hot grill for a few minutes, watching carefully so the vegetables don't burn.

FENNEL & ORANGE SALAD

I never liked fennel until I lived in Italy and tasted it raw in this salad. It's Sicilian in origin and you can use blood oranges when in season, for both taste and colour. You can replace the fennel with peeled, thinly sliced raw beetroot for an equally delicious salad. *Buon appetito!*

SERVES 4

2 fennel bulbs, about 600g, washed and dried

2 large oranges

20g raisins (optional)

1 tsp cider vinegar

5 tbsp extra-virgin olive oil

25g pine nuts, toasted (see page 127)

1 tbsp pumpkin seeds

salt

Trim the fennel, discarding the bases, cores and any tough outer layers. Cut the tops off and reserve, along with any feathery fronds. Cut the fennel in half from top to bottom and place flat side down on a chopping board. Using a sharp knife (or a mandolin), slice the fennel as thinly as possible. Transfer to a bowl of iced water and set aside until ready to serve. This will prevent browning and make it crisper.

Squeeze one orange and place the juice in a bowl. Add the raisins and leave to soak for at least 10 minutes. If you're not using raisins, keep the juice for the dressing.

Peel the other orange and cut into thin slices. (You can remove the pith, but remember that it is good for you.) Set aside.

Remove the raisins from the orange juice and set aside. Add a pinch of salt and the vinegar to the juice, then gradually whisk in the olive oil.

Place the fennel in a salad bowl with the chopped tops and fronds, orange slices, soaked raisins, toasted pine nuts and the pumpkin seeds. Add the dressing, toss gently and serve.

CARROT & ONION CHAPATIS

I was never a keen cook, but I got so fed up with the takeaways we eat living in temporary accommodation that I found myself craving home-cooked food and the tastes I had grown up with in Uganda. I started cooking my Mum's recipes and then began experimenting with my own, like this one. The Hubb Community Kitchen has been a haven for me – and it has revived my love of food.

MAKES 8 CHAPATIS

200g carrots, peeled and
  grated
300g plain flour, plus extra
  for dusting
100g onion, grated
½ tsp salt
5 tbsp vegetable oil, plus
  extra for kneading
3 tbsp ghee, or extra
  vegetable oil, for brushing

Squeeze the grated carrots between your hands to remove the juice. Reserve the juice.

Place the flour in a large mixing bowl. Add the carrots, grated onion and onion juices, salt and oil and mix to form a soft dough. Add a little of the reserved carrot juice if needed.

Knead the dough for 10 minutes, until elastic and smooth. Rub the dough with a little oil and place in a plastic bag. Set aside for about 1 hour.

Divide the dough into eight balls. Sprinkle a little flour on the work surface and roll each ball into a 17cm round.

Heat a frying pan on a low–medium heat. Dry cook each chapati for 30–40 seconds, until it starts to brown, then flip over and cook for a further 30–40 seconds. When the chapati starts to puff up, press down with a rolled clean tea towel to force the steam to escape, rotating them at the same time to avoid excessive browning. Once cooked, lightly brush both sides with ghee or oil, wrap in a tea towel and keep warm until ready to serve.

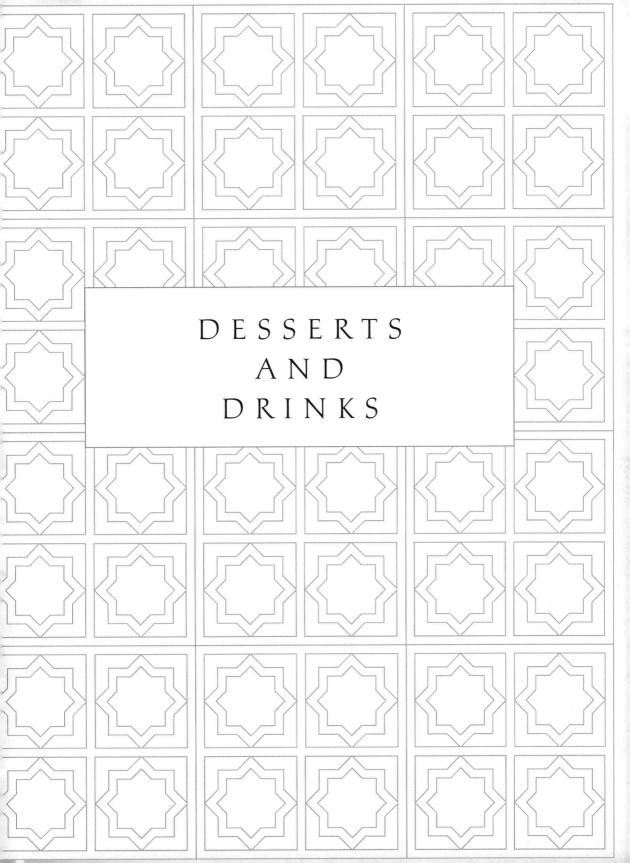

DESSERTS
AND
DRINKS

CARAMELISED PLUM UPSIDE-DOWN CAKE

✳✳✳ As soon as I heard about the Kitchen, I volunteered to help, cooking recipes from my ✳✳✳ homeland, Algeria. This cake is one my Mum used to make. She always said plums are an unreliable fruit – they can be quite sour when raw. This brings out the best in them.

SERVES 8-10

2 tsp sunflower oil,
    for greasing
300g granulated sugar
100g unsalted butter,
    very soft
½ tsp vanilla extract
¼ tsp salt
8 plums, halved and stoned
40g dark brown soft sugar
2 eggs, beaten
25g cornflour
50g ground almonds
100g plain flour
1 tsp baking powder

Preheat the oven to 170°C. Grease a 23cm round springform cake tin with the sunflower oil and place on a baking sheet.

For the caramel, put 225g of the granulated sugar into a small, wide, heavy pan on a low heat. Without stirring, let the sugar dissolve completely. Once liquid, let it gently bubble for 15–20 minutes or until it is a deep golden colour. Add 10g of the butter, half the vanilla extract and the salt, gently swirling the pan to combine the butter as it melts. Once fully incorporated, immediately remove from the heat and pour the caramel into the prepared cake tin. Place the plum halves on top, cut side down, nestled tightly together, and set aside.

In a large mixing bowl, beat the remaining butter together with the remaining granulated sugar and the brown sugar until pale and creamy: this will take 2–3 minutes using a handheld electric whisk; if you don't have one, use a wooden spoon. Add the eggs one at a time, beating well. Once the eggs are well combined, add the remaining vanilla extract, the cornflour, ground almonds, flour and baking powder to the bowl and fold through with a metal spoon until just combined (taking care not to over-mix), then pour over the plums. Smooth over the top, then bake for 40–45 minutes until cooked through: a thin skewer inserted into the centre of the cake should come out clean.

Transfer the cake to a wire rack and leave to cool in the tin for 5 minutes before turning out onto a serving plate. To do this, put the serving plate on top of the tin and flip over before releasing the sides of the tin and removing the base. Let the cake cool for a further 5 minutes before slicing.

AYSHA BORA'S *Nankhatai*

INDIAN SHORTBREAD

We're all foodies in my family. I have four daughters, ranging in age from five to 15, and we all eat together as a family every evening, sitting on the floor, talking about our day. You can serve these biscuits for breakfast, afternoon tea or as dessert. They keep for days in an airtight tin.

MAKES 40 SHORTBREAD

120g ghee
120g icing sugar
2 tbsp natural yoghurt
160g plain flour
35g gram flour
seeds from 4 cardamom
 pods (about ¼ tsp),
 coarsely ground
½ tsp baking powder
15g raw shelled pistachios,
 blitzed in a spice blender
 or food processor

Line two baking sheets with baking paper.

Put the ghee and icing sugar into a food processor and blitz until combined, about 10 seconds. Add the yoghurt and blitz again, then set aside for 10 minutes.

Meanwhile, sift the flours, cardamom seeds and baking powder into a mixing bowl. Add the flour mix to the food processor. Pulse briefly until combined, then return the mix to the bowl.

Using your hands, make 40 balls, about 10–15g each. Place the balls on the baking sheets, spaced well apart. Put the baking sheets in the fridge to chill for 20 minutes. Preheat the oven to 160°C.

Remove the baking sheets from the fridge and bake on the middle and lower shelves of the oven for 13–15 minutes, swapping them over halfway through.

Remove from the oven and immediately sprinkle the ground pistachios on top. Leave to cool on the baking sheets for 10 minutes, then transfer the shortbread to a wire rack to cool completely.

CARDAMOM BREAD & BUTTER PUDDING

When I started visiting the Hubb Kitchen, it motivated me to cook much more. My Mum is my inspiration. She was taught by her mother, but she adds her own little touches and she invented this dessert for us when I was a child. Now I make it too. My little boy is six and he loves his food; I think that's thanks to her.

SERVES 4-6

6 thick slices of white bread

225g butter

800ml whole milk

150g granulated sugar

¼ tsp ground cardamom

250ml extra-thick double cream

flaked almonds, toasted (see page 127), to decorate

Cut the bread slices in half diagonally.

Melt the butter in a small frying pan. Dip the pieces of bread in the butter to coat both sides, then fry, in batches, in a large frying pan on a medium heat for 3–4 minutes on each side, until golden. Arrange the bread in a serving dish.

Put the milk, sugar and ground cardamom in a pan and bring to the boil, then simmer for 10 minutes. Remove from the heat and leave to cool for 5 minutes.

Pour the spiced milk over the bread. Gently press the bread into the milk. Set aside for 1 hour, pressing occasionally, until all the milk has been absorbed.

Spread the cream over the top, sprinkle with the toasted flaked almonds, cover with clingfilm and chill in the fridge for at least 30 minutes before serving.

MAMA JAY AND JAY JAY'S

TOFFEE-APPLE CRUMBLE

When the mosque offered the kitchen to the community, I would come by and help out. It gives ladies a place to relax, make some home-cooked food and have a good girly catch-up. I'm not much of a one for making desserts, but I do enjoy them. This is a random concoction that I made up – it's quick and easy...I like that!

SERVES 4-6

1kg Bramley apples

2 tbsp water

200g butter, chilled and cut into small cubes

175g soft brown sugar

120ml double cream

large pinch of salt

150g plain flour

Preheat the oven to 180°C.

Peel and core the apples and cut into 3cm pieces. Place in a sauté pan with the 2 tablespoons of water, cover and cook on a medium heat for 5–6 minutes, until just soft at the edges. Transfer to a 25 x 20cm baking dish. Set aside.

Heat half of the butter cubes and 100g of the brown sugar in a heavy-based pan on a low heat for 2 minutes, until the butter has melted and the sugar has dissolved. Increase the heat to medium and leave to bubble for 5–6 minutes, stirring occasionally, until the mixture is a dark toffee colour. Add the cream and salt, taking care as it will splatter, then stir until well blended. Pour the caramel over the apples and stir to coat all the pieces.

Place the flour and the remaining butter (ensuring it is very cold) in a mixing bowl. Using your fingertips, rub the butter into the flour until the mixture looks like rough breadcrumbs. Add the remaining sugar and toss until well blended. Sprinkle the crumble over the apple mixture.

Bake for 30–35 minutes, until the top is golden and the caramel is bubbling at the edges. Leave to cool slightly before serving.

SWEET PUFF PASTRIES

I like to make most things from scratch but when it comes to puff pastry, shop-bought ready-rolled is so much quicker and easier. If you keep a pack in the freezer, you can make these pretty rose-scented pastries whenever visitors turn up.

MAKES ABOUT 15

250ml milk

3 tbsp cornflour

2 tbsp caster sugar

3 tbsp double cream

3 tbsp rose water or
   ½ tsp vanilla extract

120g cream cheese

320g ready-rolled puff pastry

1 egg, beaten

5 tbsp runny honey, or
   to taste

1 tbsp black sesame seeds or
   finely chopped pistachios

Preheat the oven to 200°C. Line a large baking sheet with baking paper.

Put the milk, cornflour and sugar in a small pan and stir until the cornflour has dissolved. Heat the mixture on a medium heat for a couple of minutes, stirring all the time and more vigorously as it thickens. Remove from the heat, stir in the cream, rose water or vanilla extract and leave to cool for 30 minutes.

Unroll the puff pastry and cut into squares (each about 7cm). Place a small amount of the rose water/vanilla mixture and cream cheese on one corner of each square then fold the other corner over to make a triangle. Seal the parcels by gently pressing the edges with the tines of a fork. Brush the tops with beaten egg and bake for 15–20 minutes or until puffed and golden.

While the puffs are still warm, drizzle with honey and sprinkle with the black sesame seeds or chopped pistachios. Serve warm or cold.

OXANA SINITSYNA'S *Mannik*

RUSSIAN SEMOLINA CAKE

Kefir is an ingredient that originated in the Caucasus Mountains. It's fermented milk – a bit like yoghurt but with a slight fizz to it – and has great health benefits, so it is now being stocked in supermarkets and health food stores. As a drink it's an acquired taste, but in this traditional cake it just adds an edge to the sweetness.

SERVES 4-6

190g coarse semolina

250g kefir

100g slightly salted butter, at room temperature, plus extra for greasing

160g dark brown soft sugar

½ tsp vanilla bean paste

2 medium eggs, beaten

1 tsp bicarbonate of soda

condensed milk, to serve (optional)

Place the semolina and kefir in a bowl and mix until well blended. Cover with a clean tea towel and leave for 2 hours.

Preheat the oven to 180°C. Butter a 20cm round cake tin.

Using a handheld electric whisk, beat the butter until soft. Add the brown sugar and whisk until creamy and slightly lighter in colour. Add the vanilla bean paste and then the beaten eggs, a little at a time, whisking thoroughly after each addition.

Gradually incorporate the semolina mixture, then the bicarbonate of soda, beating well after each addition. Pour the batter into the prepared cake tin and bake for 35 minutes, until brown and springy to the touch. Leave to cool in the tin.

Slice and serve, drizzled with condensed milk if using.

CHERINE MALLAH'S *Atayef*

RICOTTA-FILLED PANCAKES WITH ORANGE BLOSSOM SYRUP

These pancakes are filled with a mix of ricotta, orange blossom syrup and crushed pistachios and they are a traditional dessert often served at Ramadan. However, we like to eat them all year round, as they are also very light and lower in fat than most desserts.

MAKES 12

For the batter
150g fine semolina
75g self-raising flour
3.5g fast-action dried yeast
(half of a 7g sachet)
½ tsp baking powder
1 tsp caster sugar
pinch of salt
375ml warm water

For the syrup
100g caster sugar
125ml water
2 tbsp orange blossom water

For the filling
250g ricotta
3 tbsp syrup (from above)
25g shelled pistachios,
crushed

Put all the ingredients for the batter in a large mixing bowl and thoroughly whisk to combine. Cover loosely with clingfilm and set aside to rise for 45 minutes.

Meanwhile, make the syrup. Heat the sugar, water and orange blossom water in a small pan on a low heat until the sugar has dissolved, about 5 minutes. Increase the heat and boil for about 10 minutes, until the mixture reaches a syrup consistency. Transfer to a small bowl and leave to cool.

Heat a non-stick frying pan on a low–medium heat; when it's hot, add a small ladleful of batter to the pan. Cook the pancake for 3–4 minutes, until the surface has lots of bubbles and has dried. Do not flip; transfer straight to kitchen paper and repeat with the rest of the batter, making a total of 12 pancakes. Set aside, but do not stack them or they may stick together.

When you have made all the pancakes, prepare the filling. Mix the ricotta with 3 tablespoons of the cooled syrup. Hold one pancake in the palm of your hand and add 1 tablespoon of the ricotta mix in the centre. Bring the edges of the pancake together and press firmly along the edges to seal the pancake until you reach the centre – leaving half the pancake open. Sprinkle crushed pistachios on the exposed ricotta filling and set aside. Fill the remaining pancakes in the same way.

Serve with the remaining syrup alongside.

SIMPLE CHOCOLATE CAKE

☼ I got this recipe from my sister Linda, who lives in France. It's a family favourite and was one of the first things I brought in when I started coming to the Kitchen. Then I kept getting messages from the women saying 'bring more chocolate cake next time'. It's very easy and always works. If I'm in a hurry I don't always bother with icing, but if you do, it's special enough for a birthday cake. I decorate it with chocolate buttons and little biscuits for the kids and they love it.

SERVES 4-6

125g dark chocolate,
    roughly chopped
3 tbsp milk
125g self-raising flour
3 tbsp cocoa powder
150g butter, at room
    temperature, plus extra
    for greasing
150g caster sugar
3 eggs, beaten

For the icing
75g butter, at room
    temperature
1 tbsp double cream
1 tsp vanilla extract
175g icing sugar
1 tbsp cocoa powder, plus
    extra for dusting

Preheat the oven to 150°C. Butter and line the base of a 20cm round cake tin with baking paper.

Place the chocolate and milk in a heatproof bowl and set over a pan of barely simmering water, ensuring that the bottom of the bowl does not touch the water. Once melted, leave to cool slightly.

Sift the flour and cocoa powder together. Set aside.

Using a handheld electric whisk, beat the butter until soft. Add the caster sugar and whisk until creamy and light. Add the beaten eggs a little at a time, whisking thoroughly after each addition.

Using a metal spoon, fold in the melted chocolate and then the flour and cocoa mixture until just combined, without over-mixing the batter. Pour into the prepared tin, smooth the top and bake for about 35–40 minutes, or until a skewer inserted into the centre of the cake comes out clean. Leave to cool completely in the tin, before turning out.

To make the icing, whisk the butter together with the cream and vanilla extract, then gradually add the icing sugar and cocoa powder, whisking until the mixture is soft and fluffy.

Spread the icing on top of the cake and dust lightly with cocoa powder. Alternatively, you can slice the cake in half horizontally and sandwich the two halves together with half of the icing, then spread the rest on top.

SANNA MIRZA'S

MASALA CHAI

 This cinnamon-flavoured tea is an infusion of many flavours and has many health benefits. It is a much-loved treat, especially in Pakistan and India.

SERVES 4

2cm piece of fresh root
    ginger
6 green cardamom pods
700ml water
300ml whole milk
1 cinnamon stick
¼ tsp crushed black pepper
2 tbsp loose black tea leaves
2 tbsp sugar, or to taste

Peel and finely chop the ginger and slightly crush the cardamom pods under the blade of a knife.

Put the water, milk, ginger and spices in a pan. Bring to the boil, reduce the heat and simmer for 10 minutes, stirring all the time to prevent the milk from boiling over.

Add the tea leaves and sugar, stir and simmer for another 5 minutes.

Strain into mugs or heatproof glasses and serve.

MUNIRA MAHMUD'S

GINGER TEA

In Uganda we drink ginger tea all the time. It's very refreshing and at its simplest it's just fresh ginger, grated and steeped in water. We say the richer you are, the more spices you put in. This is the way I like it, but you can add more – or fewer – spices.

SERVES 4

60g fresh root ginger
6 green cardamom pods
1 cinnamon stick
¼ tsp ground black pepper
5 cloves
1 star anise
800ml water
sugar, to taste

Peel and grate the ginger and slightly crush the cardamom pods under the blade of a knife.

Place all the spices in a pan and cover with the water. Bring to the boil, reduce the heat and simmer for 15 minutes.

Strain into mugs or heatproof glasses, add sugar to taste and serve.

SPICED MINT TEA

*** This reminds me of my Dad. We used to have it in little glasses with gold rims, and he would lift the pot up and down as he poured so we could see the pale green tea streaming out. I don't put a lot of sugar in my version, but Dad drank his honey-sweet! *Pictured on page 121.*

SERVES 4

15g fresh mint

1 clove

1 cinnamon stick

½ tsp sugar (optional)

700ml boiling water

Place the mint and spices (and sugar if using) in a teapot and pour in the boiling water. Leave to infuse for 5 minutes, then serve in small tea cups or heatproof glasses.

THE ROYAL FOUNDATION

Together has been created with help from The Royal Foundation, which is the primary philanthropic and charitable vehicle for The Duke and Duchess of Cambridge and The Duke and Duchess of Sussex.

The work of The Royal Foundation is driven by a desire to make a difference together. The charity focuses on bringing people together and developing innovative projects that will bring lasting change around issues that matter to society, and which Their Royal Highnesses are passionate about.

The Duchess of Sussex and The Royal Foundation have worked with the women of the Hubb Community Kitchen since early 2018 to create *Together*.

Profits from the sales of this charitable book will support the Hubb Community Kitchen, keeping it open for up to seven days a week, helping widen its reach to others in the community, and enabling it to continue transforming lives and communities through the power of cooking.

The Royal Foundation is administering the transfer of funds from the sale of *Together* to the Hubb Community Kitchen.

For more information about the kitchen please visit:

www.royalfoundation.com/together-cookbook

COOKING IN THE COMMUNITY

We hope that you've enjoyed cooking and eating the delicious recipes that fill each page of this book. Every special dish included in *Together* comes from the women of the Hubb Community Kitchen; whether it be a family favourite passed down through generations, or a newer creation trialled to perfection, all the recipes work because they have been cooked with love.

Every dish tells a unique story of history, culture and family, personally introduced by the women on each page. These memories remind us that *Together* is more than a cookbook; it is a storybook of a West London community and how the act of cooking together has helped them to connect, heal and look forward. At the heart of this book is the message that a simple, shared dish can create connections between people, restore hope and normality, and provide a sense of home – wherever you may be in the world.

If *Together* has inspired you, we'd love to hear about it. You may already cook within your community, or cooking and sharing food has helped you or others through a time of adversity. Perhaps swapping much-loved recipes has brought you closer to your neighbours and helped to celebrate diversity in your community. Or maybe you simply have a special memory of a particular dish that is meaningful to you.

If, like us, you are passionate about how food can tell a story and bring people together, we would love to hear from you. Connect with us at:

TogetherCookBook@royalfoundation.com

www.royalfoundation.com/together-cookbook

#CookTogether

COOKERY NOTES

Oven temperatures are for fan ovens.

Eggs are organic and medium unless otherwise specified.

All spoon measurements are level. 1 teaspoon = 5ml; 1 tablespoon = 15ml.

To toast nuts: scatter on a baking sheet and toast in a 140°C oven for 3–4 minutes until golden and aromatic.

10 9 8 7 6 5 4 3 2

Ebury Press, an imprint of Ebury Publishing
20 Vauxhall Bridge Road,
London SW1V 2SA

Ebury Press is part of the Penguin
Random House group of companies
whose addresses can be found at global.
penguinrandomhouse.com

THE ROYAL FOUNDATION

First published by Ebury Press in 2018
www.penguin.co.uk

A CIP catalogue record for this book is
available from the British Library

ISBN 978-1-52910-292-5

Publishing Director: Lizzy Gray
Project Editor: Emily Preece-Morrison
Photographer: Jenny Zarins
Designer: David Eldridge at Two Associates
Food Stylists and Recipe Testers: Valerie
Berry and Megan Davies
Prop Stylist: Tabitha Hawkins
Writer (additional text): Lindsay Nicholson
Copy Editor: Maggie Ramsay

Colour origination by Altaimage, London
Printed and bound in Germany by
Mohn Media GmbH

MIX
Paper from
responsible sources
FSC® C018179

With thanks to:
Gail Rebuck, Rebecca Smart, Joe Stone,
Kate Parker, Hilary Bird, Helen Everson,
Lucy Harrison, Louise McKeever,
Lee Jenkins, Rob King, Tim Norman,
the team at Mohn Media, Leila Hedjem,
Cherine Mallah, Oxana Sinitsyna,
Munira Mahmud, Halima Al-Hudafi,
Intlak Alsaiegh, Aysha Bora,
Faiza Hayani Bellili, Claren Bilal,
Amaal Abd Elrasoul, Sanna Mirza,
Ahlam Saeid, Jay Jay, Gurmit Kaur,
Hiwot Dagnachew, Jennifer Fatima Odonkor,
Dayo Gilmour, Lillian Olwa, Honey Akhter,
Zahira Ghaswala, the Al-Manaar Muslim
Cultural Heritage Centre.